SELECTED SHORTER POEMS OF

THOMAS HARDY

SELECTED SHORTER POEMS OF

THOMAS HARDY

CHOSEN AND INTRODUCED BY

JOHN WAIN

M

Selection and editorial matter © John Wain 1966, 1975
Typography © Macmillan London 1966, 1975

ISBN 0 333 05906 9

First published 1966 [as Papermac P.157]
Revised edition 1975
Reprinted 1976 (twice), 1977, 1980, 1981

Published by
MACMILLAN LONDON LIMITED
London and Basingstoke

*Associated companies in Auckland, Dallas,
Delhi, Dublin, Hong Kong, Johannesburg,
Lagos, Manzini, Melbourne, Nairobi,
New York, Singapore, Tokyo, Washington
and Zaria*

Printed in Hong Kong by
C.T.P.S.

CONTENTS

Time's Laughingstocks and Other Verses

Time's Laughingstocks

Satires of Circumstance

Lyrics and Reveries

Late Lyrics and Earlier

Human Shows, Far Phantasies, Songs, and Trifles

Winter Words in Various Moods and Metres

INTRODUCTION

THOMAS HARDY was, constitutionally and by inclination, primarily a poet. Had he possessed private means, it is doubtful whether he would have written novels at all, though once he had turned his hand to prose fiction he went on, in his usual strong and steady way, until he had produced a body of work considerable enough to win respect all over the world. Nevertheless, it was poetry that first drew him towards the idea of being a writer. His second wife, Florence Emily Hardy, in *The Early Life of Thomas Hardy* (the first of two fat biographical volumes which are thought to have been written up from material dictated by Hardy himself), gives us a glimpse of the young man, serving his apprenticeship to architecture in a London office, and doggedly pursuing the path of a poet despite disappointment and rejection slips:

> '... he did not by any means abandon verse, which he wrote constantly, but kept private, through the years 1866 and most of 1867, resolving to send no more poetry to magazines whose editors probably did not know good poetry from bad, and forming meanwhile the quixotic opinion that, as in verse was concentrated the essence of all imaginative and emotional literature, to read verse and nothing else was the shortest way to the fountain-head of such, for one who had not a great deal of spare time. And in fact for nearly or quite two years he did not read a word of prose except such as came under his eye in the daily newspapers and weekly reviews.'

Just what is 'quixotic' in the young Hardy's decision to give all his reading time to poetry, I do not know. It seems to me an excellent piece of common sense, much to be recommended to any young person who wants to acquire an insight into the nature of imaginative writing without taking years over the job. To know English poetry well is to see the richest and most intense workings of the English imagination, whereas to know only English fiction or drama would not only take longer but be less rewarding. And for 'English' read 'French' or (I suspect) any other nationality, certainly in Europe.

These two years of reading the English poets must have been invaluable for Hardy's development as a writer, whether of verse or prose. But prose, for practical reasons, carried the day. For twenty-five years he worked as a novelist — not, indeed, to the total exclusion of poetry, for which he always tried to reserve some of his time and energy. But poetry cannot be written in one's 'spare time', or fed on the energy left when other work has consumed its share. After that quarter-century of effort, Hardy took off his novelist's hat and hung it up for good. The hostility which, in many quarters, greeted *Jude the Obscure* (1895) appears to have sickened him with the novel-reading public, and after one more prose story (*The Well-Beloved*, 1897) he settled down to spend the rest of his life, supported in modest comfort by the royalties from his novels, writing what he really wanted to write: narrative, dramatic, and lyric poetry.

As a poet, Hardy not unnaturally works over the same themes that we find in his prose. His work is concerned mainly with suffering, and in particular with the human sense of impotence in the face of a ruthless destiny. He described himself as an agnostic, but he was in many ways closer to being an atheist in the high Victorian manner, combining disbelief in God with a venomous dislike of Him for not existing. The strength of Hardy's work comes mainly from a tragic stoicism, a blind will to go on living in despite of the malignancy of fate; and also from a considerable curiosity about human nature. Much has been made of Hardy's affinities with Browning, but it seems to me that if he owes anything to any previous poet that poet is Wordsworth, and in particular the Wordsworth of the 'Lucy' and 'Matthew' poems, where he is interested in presenting, without comment or analysis, the odd quirks of the human mind under the pressure of life; so that poems like 'The Two April Mornings' or 'Strange Fits of Passion Have I Known' lead directly to the Hardy of 'In Her Precincts' or 'The Self-Unseeing'. Already in 1868 Hardy was writing in his notebook, 'Perhaps I can do a volume of poems consisting of the *other side* of common emotions.' To view everyday experience from an unusual angle and give the unexpected insight — this was his aim as it was Wordsworth's. They are both poets of normality. But they both understand that normality is not the simple thing it was once supposed.

Another resemblance between Hardy and Wordsworth is that they both had the same knack of slipping in and out of autobiography. Hardy's utter unselfconsciousness in this respect is one of the most interesting features of his work. He builds his poem round a story or a situation, and it appears to make no difference whether the original event happened to him, or to someone else, or just occurred to his imagination. Many poets feel a need to cover their tracks elaborately when speaking of their own experience or situation; others are so compulsively autobiographical that they must re-tell every story, or shape every invention, to put themselves at the centre. Hardy simply goes ahead with what comes to hand. Some of his meditative lyrics deal very directly with his own experience; for instance, the rush of poems that flowed out of his grief at the death of his first wife in 1912 — a grief inflamed by remorse, for their relationship had been a stormy one. Others start from experiences that might, or might not, have been Hardy's own. But his poetic practice is not affected one way or the other. He is entirely pragmatic, working to no theory of self-expression or self-concealment. One feels that Hardy would have scarcely understood a sophisticated distinction like T. S. Eliot's 'Poetry is not a turning loose of emotion, but an escape from emotion; it is not the expression of personality, but an escape from personality' — not because he lacked the intelligence to understand it, but because he would have seen no need to draw such careful diagrams.

Stylistically, as in theme, Hardy's poetry is remarkably consistent. He evidently made up his mind very early as to the kind of music he wanted to play on the great keyboard of the English language, and there is hardly any difference in texture and movement between his early poems, written in the seventies and eighties, and those of half a century later. In contrast to this steady consistency of diction there is, of course, his incessant switching of metrical forms. He is for ever varying rhyme-scheme and length of line; if any-one had the patience to go through all the poems Hardy published and count the number of different verse-forms he used, the total would be higher, I should guess, than in the case of any other English poet. And many of these forms must have been of Hardy's own devising. Not that we need, on these grounds alone, bestow on him the title of 'experi-mental' poet. To vary one's stanza restlessly from poem to poem, to switch from exceedingly short lines to exceedingly long ones, is not experimentation : it probes hardly at all into the nature of poetic effect : nor did Hardy intend it to probe. It reminds us more of the work of a village craftsman who makes tables and chairs, beds and sofas, adapting the shape of each one to fit a different set of circumstances, but always using the same basic local materials.

And indeed Hardy's poems are very like the work of a village craftsman, just as he himself, in appearance and manner, seems to have resembled such a man. ('They say he looks like a little old stone-mason,' wrote Robert Frost to an American friend in 1913.) Like a rural workman, he built plainly and built to last, with no factory-tooled precision but with each new object shaped by the living hand to fit into its own special place. His language is not elegant, his lines do not flow smoothly; when he sets himself a difficult

metrical task and carries it out with a skill born of long
practice, the result is never slick or varnished. There is always
a certain stiff deliberation, the unhurried gait of the country
man going about his immemorial business.

Take any typical stanza :

> You were she who abode
> By those red-veined rocks far West,
> You were the swan-necked one who rode
> Along the beetling Beeny Crest,
> And, reining nigh me,
> Would muse and eye me,
> While Life unrolled us its very best.

So he thinks, after his wife's death, of their happiest times
together, many years earlier. The verse moves one plodding
step at a time, with no rhythmical *élan* : the rhymes are
matter-of-fact, as if the poet had merely set himself to find
certain words that chimed together and had, so to speak,
fulfilled his contract when he had lit on them. But highly-
finished writing would not be able to convey the feeling that
this poem, and the others like it, seek to convey. The plain-
ness, the awkwardness, the crick in the neck, the creak of
boots, all heighten the impression of ordinariness, of the in-
evitable suffering of an unremarkable life, and it is this
impression that makes the poems so moving. This conscious
plainness, this beautiful clumsiness, are as much in evidence
in Hardy's most famous and successful poems as in his run-
of-the-mill output.

> They throw in Drummer Hodge, to rest
> Uncoffined — just as found :
> His landmark is a kopje-crest
> That breaks the veldt around;
> And foreign constellations west
> Each night above his mound.

Or, again, the first line of one of the most purely beautiful of all his poems, 'Afterwards':

When the Present has latched its postern behind my
tremulous stay . . .

Here, the movement of the line is slow, wavering, well suited to its function of suggesting the movements of an old man, slowly walking off the stage of life. Or some old family servant, closing and fastening the postern gate, on a summer's night, behind some departing visitor. The final 's' of 'tremulous', coming immediately before the initial 's' of 'stay', is the sort of double hiss an accomplished verse-writer would avoid (not many of them, I imagine, could be found in Tennyson), yet this slight awkwardness gives the right impression of unpolished, hesitant sincerity.

In fact 'Afterwards' will repay pondering for a number of reasons. It is a poem of thanksgiving: a benediction on the things that have brought happiness during life. Hardy's view of human existence was harsh and gloomy; he speaks of 'the monotonous moils of strained, hard-run Humanity', and as a writer what chiefly interests him is how the stuff of human character is affected by the endless strains to which a hostile destiny subjects it: how people break up, or warp out of shape, or harden into an inflexible bitter defiance. On the other hand, if we compare him with two other poets of the tragic vision, working during the same years, we see that he is very much his own man. W. B. Yeats and A. E. Housman were both poets who took the view that the human condition is tragic: Yeats expressed it with a kind of fierce joy which accepted tragedy but rejected drab submissiveness; he felt that though we time-bound creatures had to go down before our fate, we must go down with banners flying and guns firing; he knew that 'Hamlet and Lear are gay'. Housman, for his part, gives the impression of perceiving the human tragedy through the windows of a room lined with books and classical busts; beautiful and memorable as his poems are, they are always the utterances of a literary man, distilled by a patient art rather than forced out by the pressure and impact of life. If we come to Hardy after these two other great poets we see at once that we are in the presence of what can only be called a peasant view of life. Hardy has the peasant's realism, his grim resignation to the fact that life will be harsh, that the best part of it will be over soon and after that the years will bear heavily down. But he also has the dour humour, the relish for an odd tale about his neighbour, and the slow endurance that carries on in spite of all. He resents the cruelty of fate, but he would never, like Housman, rail against

> Whatever brute or blackguard made the world;

there is a kind of petulance in such railing, and the peasant is never petulant: he has the patience and silent strength of an animal. So, in 'Afterwards', we see the essential countryman, who does not praise the beauty of the countryside, but immerses himself in its slow, fruitful rhythms and enjoys, hardly knowing that he is enjoying them, the common sights and sounds: the hedgehog 'travelling furtively over the lawn', the 'full-starred heavens that winter sees', the church bells whose sound is now carried, now interrupted, by the wind. And the only epitaph the poet wants is that he 'used to notice such things'; he was unobtrusively there, part of the scene, taking note of it all. Housman, in his great hymn to the beauty of rural Nature, 'Tell me not here, it needs not saying', had been careful to dissociate himself from any over-eager sense of 'involvement' with her:

> For nature, heartless, witless nature,
>   Will neither care nor know
> What stranger's feet may find the meadow
>   And trespass there and go,

> Nor ask amid the dews of morning
> If they are mine or no.

This is the literary man's reaction, using the Pathetic Fallacy to deny the truth of the Pathetic Fallacy. Hardy, by contrast, seems indifferent, as a peasant would be, to whether he is 'at one' with Nature or not. He was there, he moved among these scenes not as a 'trespasser' but as one who lived there by habitual right; he 'used to notice such things'; that is all. And what, finally, gives him the strength to live in spite of the gloominess of his world-view is his sense, again peasant-like, of a steadily moving life which goes forward, day after day, in obedience to the overarching will of Nature, and which without effort includes and transcends all our petty struggles and contrivances. The man harrowing clods, the thin blue smoke from a bonfire, the whispering of the young couple,

> this will go onward the same
> Though Dynasties pass.

Then again, like anyone who understands a toilsome and monotonous life, Hardy has a great weakness for junketings and good times; the rather roguish gaiety that suddenly flashes out from 'Great Things', or the not very innocent fun of 'The Ruined Maid', are all part of the countryman's reaction to life. So, for that matter, is the flinty hardness of his satire. When Hardy lashes out in sudden anger, it is like a blow from a navvy's fist. Many writers have attacked the folly of war, but no poem tramples it more swiftly and more thoroughly than 'I Looked Up From My Writing'.

For these reasons we may speak of Hardy as a rural poet, who sees things as the peasant has always seen them. At the same time, we must not fall into the trap of seeing him as a poet of direct vision and technical simplicity who has at his command nothing else but this directness and simplicity. He was, to be sure, innocent of the obliquity which has so strongly characterised modern poetry and modern art in general. He liked to speak of 'irony', but in fact his own ironies are so transparent and predictable that they come across as Arcadian straightforwardness. Still, he was also a genuine artist, and an artist always has his stratagems and his subtle involvements. Hardy's language, as we have noted, gives the impression of a plain man struggling to speak the awkward truths in his mind. But very often, if we examine this language, we shall find that under the clumping earnestness there is a richness and cunning. Take, for instance, the lines:

> Portion of this yew
> Is a man my grandsire knew,
> Bosomed here at its foot.

The word *bosomed*, there, sounds rustic and old-fashioned, which is appropriate when the subject of the poem is a man's musings in a simple country churchyard. It is only when we try to disentangle the strands that we realise how many there are. The dead man is buried at the root of the yew tree; he is *bosomed* in the earth, held closely in her heart: the word *bosom* implies secrecy and also fondness ('bosom friends', 'secrets of my bosom'). The earth shows love for the dead man, admits him to her innermost sanctuary, allows him to partake in the sacred process of the renewal of life, in this case the life of a tree but no less life for that. By its sound, the word *bosom* may also smuggle into our minds, subliminally, the suggestion of *blossom*. Then there is the visual effect. Most people see an image when they read a statement; admittedly these things are to some extent subjective, but in my case at any rate the image that arises is of the man lying beneath the soil with the roots of the tree coming out of his chest; his heart, traditionally the seat of life and the seat of the vital emotions, is sending its accumulated experience upward into the tree's trunk; it grows from his bosom, like the 'Southern tree' from Drummer Hodge's 'breast and brain'. If we were to re-write the line as '*buried* here at its root', we should still be conveying the basic sense, but the richness of suggestion would be lost. And that richness is to be found surprisingly often in Hardy's poetry.

Perhaps this is why, in addition to his strong fascination for the ordinary non-professional reader, Hardy's poetry has always interested other poets. His influence on subsequent poetry has been unspectacular yet persistent. In our reading of twentieth-century poetry, we are constantly coming across echoes and parallels. Robert Frost's 'Death of the Hired Man' is exactly the kind of narrative poem (or, more precisely, situation-poem) that Hardy delighted in; while poems like John Betjeman's 'On a Portrait of a Deaf Man' or Philip Larkin's 'Love Songs in Age' would probably not have come out quite as they did if Hardy had never existed.

Hardy's long life coincided with a time of neglect for poetry. The industrial, urbanised society that developed in the later nineteenth century was, as far as the arts were concerned, a ruthless leveller. It gathered information rapidly and in huge quantities; with the aid of the electric telegraph and the mechanical printing-press it developed the daily newspaper and the inexpensive pamphlet; by uprooting people from their homes, it destroyed the continuity in which fable and tradition survive; and by encouraging the habit of rapid, silent reading, necessary to keep up with the enormous increase in letterpress, it weighted the scales against any form of writing that needs the speaking voice. It preferred literature in a homely, realistic vein; its great love was the matter-of-fact novel. A good many people were completely mystified by the fact that Hardy, at the height of his reputation, abandoned prose fiction and devoted the last thirty years of his life to poetry. (I suspect, from various remarks she lets drop, that his second wife was among them.) To such observers, it looked as if he were turning away from serious (and profit-making) work to pursue an idle hobby.

Now that poetry has survived that long winter, and come back into something like its own, Hardy's recognition of his own deep compulsion to write in verse seems only natural and commendable. He was always bitter about the current neglect of the art he loved most. 'The poet,' he wrote in 1918, 'is like one who enters and mounts a platform to give an address as announced. He opens his page, looks around, and finds the hall — *empty*.' But many things have happened in the years since that complaint was uttered. And one of them is that the hall has quietly been filling up. Let us take our seats with the others, and listen to the voice of a man whose deepest wish was to be a major English poet, who toiled at his art so devotedly that he has left us nearly a thousand examples of it; none of them quite without interest, and some of them fit to rank with the greatest achievements of modern lyric verse.

JOHN WAIN

WESSEX POEMS AND
OTHER VERSES

NEUTRAL TONES

W E stood by a pond that winter day,
And the sun was white, as though chidden of God,
And a few leaves lay on the starving sod;
    — They had fallen from an ash, and were gray.

Your eyes on me were as eyes that rove
Over tedious riddles of years ago;
And some words played between us to and fro
    On which lost the more by our love.

The smile on your mouth was the deadest thing
Alive enough to have strength to die;
And a grin of bitterness swept thereby
    Like an ominous bird a-wing. . . .

Since then, keen lessons that love deceives,
And wrings with wrong, have shaped to me
Your face, and the God-curst sun, and a tree,
    And a pond edged with grayish leaves.

    1867.

SHE AT HIS FUNERAL

THEY bear him to his resting-place —
In slow procession sweeping by;
I follow at a stranger's space;
His kindred they, his sweetheart I.

Unchanged my gown of garish dye,
Though sable-sad is their attire;
But they stand round with griefless eye,
Whilst my regret consumes like fire!

187–.

SHE, TO HIM

I

WHEN you shall see me in the toils of Time,
My lauded beauties carried off from me,
My eyes no longer stars as in their prime,
My name forgot of Maiden Fair and Free;

When, in your being, heart concedes to mind,
And judgment, though you scarce its process know,
Recalls the excellencies I once enshrined,
And you are irked that they have withered so:

Remembering mine the loss is, not the blame,
That Sportsman Time but rears his brood to kill,
Knowing me in my soul the very same —
One who would die to spare you touch of ill! —
Will you not grant to old affection's claim
The hand of friendship down Life's sunless hill?

1866.

SHE, TO HIM

II

PERHAPS, long hence, when I have passed away,
Some other's feature, accent, thought like mine,
Will carry you back to what I used to say,
And bring some memory of your love's decline.

Then you may pause awhile and think, 'Poor jade!'
And yield a sigh to me — as ample due,
Not as the tittle of a debt unpaid
To one who could resign her all to you —

And thus reflecting, you will never see
That your thin thought, in two small words conveyed,
Was no such fleeting phantom-thought to me,
But the Whole Life wherein my part was played;
And you amid its fitful masquerade
A Thought — as I in your life seem to be!

    1866.

SHE, TO HIM

III

I WILL be faithful to thee; aye, I will!
And Death shall choose me with a wondering eye
That he did not discern and domicile
One his by right ever since that last Good-bye!

I have no care for friends, or kin, or prime
Of manhood who deal gently with me here;
Amid the happy people of my time
Who work their love's fulfilment, I appear

Numb as a vane that cankers on its point,
True to the wind that kissed ere canker came:
Despised by souls of Now, who would disjoint
The mind from memory, making Life all aim,

My old dexterities in witchery gone,
And nothing left for Love to look upon.

    1866.

SHE, TO HIM

IV

THIS love puts all humanity from me;
I can but maledict her, pray her dead,
For giving love and getting love of thee —
Feeding a heart that else mine own had fed!

How much I love I know not, life not known,
Save as one unit I would add love by;
But this I know, my being is but thine own —
Fused from its separateness by ecstasy.

And thus I grasp thy amplitudes, of her
Ungrasped, though helped by nigh-regarding eyes;
Canst thou then hate me as an envier
Who see unrecked what I so dearly prize?
Believe me, Lost One, Love is lovelier
The more it shapes its moan in selfish-wise.

   1866.

NATURE'S QUESTIONING

WHEN I look forth at dawning, pool,
     Field, flock, and lonely tree,
     All seem to gaze at me
Like chastened children sitting silent in a school;

Their faces dulled, constrained, and worn,
     As though the master's ways
     Through the long teaching days
Had cowed them till their early zest was overborne.

Upon them stirs in lippings mere
    (As if once clear in call,
    But now scarce breathed at all) —
'We wonder, ever wonder, why we find us here!

    'Has some Vast Imbecility,
        Mighty to build and blend,
        But impotent to tend,
Framed us in jest, and left us now to hazardry?

    'Or come we of an Automaton
        Unconscious of our pains? . . .
        Or are we live remains
Of Godhead dying downwards, brain and eye now gone?

    'Or is it that some high Plan betides,
        As yet not understood,
        Of Evil stormed by Good,
We the Forlorn Hope over which Achievement strides?'

    Thus things around. No answerer I . . .
        Meanwhile the winds, and rains,
        And Earth's old glooms and pains
Are still the same, and Life and Death are neighbours nigh.

'I LOOK INTO MY GLASS'

I LOOK into my glass,
And view my wasting skin,
And say, 'Would God it came to pass
My heart had shrunk as thin!'

For then, I, undistrest
By hearts grown cold to me,
Could lonely wait my endless rest
With equanimity.

But Time, to make me grieve,
Part steals, lets part abide;
And shakes this fragile frame at eve
With throbbings of noontide.

POEMS OF THE PAST
AND THE PRESENT

WAR POEMS

DRUMMER HODGE

I

THEY throw in Drummer Hodge, to rest
    Uncoffined — just as found :
His landmark is a kopje-crest
    That breaks the veldt around;
And foreign constellations west
    Each night above his mound.

II

Young Hodge the Drummer never knew —
    Fresh from his Wessex home —
The meaning of the broad Karoo,
    The Bush, the dusty loam,
And why uprose to nightly view
    Strange stars amid the gloam.

III

Yet portion of that unknown plain
    Will Hodge for ever be;
His homely Northern breast and brain
    Grow to some Southern tree,
And strange-eyed constellations reign
    His stars eternally.

POEMS OF PILGRIMAGE

SHELLEY'S SKYLARK

(The neighbourhood of Leghorn: March 1887)

SOMEWHERE afield here something lies
In Earth's oblivious eyeless trust
That moved a poet to prophecies —
A pinch of unseen, unguarded dust:

The dust of the lark that Shelley heard,
And made immortal through times to be; —
Though it only lived like another bird,
And knew not its immortality:

Lived its meek life; then, one day, fell —
A little ball of feather and bone;
And how it perished, when piped farewell,
And where it wastes, are alike unknown.

Maybe it rests in the loam I view,
Maybe it throbs in a myrtle's green,
Maybe it sleeps in the coming hue
Of a grape on the slopes of yon inland scene.

Go find it, faeries, go and find
That tiny pinch of priceless dust,
And bring a casket silver-lined,
And framed of gold that gems encrust;

12

And we will lay it safe therein,
And consecrate it to endless time;
For it inspired a bard to win
Ecstatic heights in thought and rhyme.

MISCELLANEOUS POEMS

AT A LUNAR ECLIPSE

THY shadow, Earth, from Pole to Central Sea,
Now steals along upon the Moon's meek shine
In even monochrome and curving line
Of imperturbable serenity.

How shall I link such sun-cast symmetry
With the torn troubled form I know as thine,
That profile, placid as a brow divine,
With continents of moil and misery?

And can immense Mortality but throw
So small a shade, and Heaven's high human scheme
Be hemmed within the coasts yon arc implies?

Is such the stellar gauge of earthly show,
Nation at war with nation, brains that teem,
Heroes, and women fairer than the skies?

TO AN UNBORN PAUPER CHILD

I

BREATHE not, hid Heart : cease silently,
And though thy birth-hour beckons thee,
    Sleep the long sleep :
    The Doomsters heap
Travails and teens around us here,
And Time-wraiths turn our songsingings to fear.

II

Hark, how the peoples surge and sigh,
And laughters fail, and greetings die:
    Hopes dwindle; yea,
    Faiths waste away,
Affections and enthusiasms numb;
Thou canst not mend these things if thou dost come.

III

Had I the ear of wombèd souls
Ere their terrestrial chart unrolls,
    And thou wert free
    To cease, or be,
Then would I tell thee all I know,
And put it to thee: Wilt thou take Life so?

IV

Vain vow! No hint of mine may hence
To theeward fly: to thy locked sense
    Explain none can
    Life's pending plan:
Thou wilt thy ignorant entry make
Though skies spout fire and blood and nations quake.

V

Fain would I, dear, find some shut plot
Of earth's wide wold for thee, where not
    One tear, one qualm,
    Should break the calm.
But I am weak as thou and bare;
No man can change the common lot to rare.

VI

Must come and bide. And such are we —
Unreasoning, sanguine, visionary —
    That I can hope
    Health, love, friends, scope
In full for thee; can dream thou'lt find
Joys seldom yet attained by humankind!

TO LIZBIE BROWNE

I

DEAR Lizbie Browne,
Where are you now?
In sun, in rain?—
Or is your brow
Past joy, past pain,
Dear Lizbie Browne?

II

Sweet Lizbie Browne,
How you could smile,
How you could sing!—
How archly wile
In glance-giving,
Sweet Lizbie Browne!

III

And, Lizbie Browne,
Who else had hair
Bay-red as yours,
Or flesh so fair
Bred out of doors,
Sweet Lizbie Browne?

IV

When, Lizbie Browne,
You had just begun
To be endeared
By stealth to one,
You disappeared,
My Lizbie Browne!

V

Ay, Lizbie Browne,
So swift your life,
And mine so slow,
You were a wife
Ere I could show
Love, Lizbie Browne.

VI

Still, Lizbie Browne,
You won, they said,
The best of men
When you were wed. . . .
Where went you then,
O Lizbie Browne?

VII

Dear Lizbie Browne,
I should have thought,
'Girls ripen fast,'
And coaxed and caught
You ere you passed,
Dear Lizbie Browne!

VIII

But, Lizbie Browne,
I let you slip;
Shaped not a sign;
Touched never your lip
With lip of mine,
Lost Lizbie Browne!

IX

So, Lizbie Browne,
When on a day
Men speak of me
As not, you'll say,
'And who was he?'—
Yes, Lizbie Browne!

A BROKEN APPOINTMENT

You did not come,
And marching Time drew on, and wore me numb.—
Yet less for loss of your dear presence there
Than that I thus found lacking in your make
That high compassion which can overbear
Reluctance for pure lovingkindness' sake
Grieved I, when, as the hope-hour stroked its sum,
You did not come.

You love not me,
And love alone can lend you loyalty;
— I know and knew it. But, unto the store
Of human deeds divine in all but name,
Was it not worth a little hour or more
To add yet this: Once you, a woman, came
To soothe a time-torn man; even though it be
You love not me?

HIS IMMORTALITY

I

I SAW a dead man's finer part
Shining within each faithful heart
Of those bereft. Then said I : 'This must be
    His immortality.'

II

I looked there as the seasons wore,
And still his soul continuously bore
A life in theirs. But less its shine excelled
    Than when I first beheld.

III

His fellow-yearsmen passed, and then
In later hearts I looked for him again;
And found him — shrunk, alas! into a thin
    And spectral mannikin.

IV

Lastly I ask — now old and chill —
If aught of him remain unperished still;
And find, in me alone, a feeble spark,
    Dying amid the dark.

February 1899.

THE PUZZLED GAME-BIRDS

(TRIOLET)

THEY are not those who used to feed us
When we were young — they cannot be —

These shapes that now bereave and bleed us?
They are not those who used to feed us,
For did we then cry, they would heed us
— If hearts can house such treachery
They are not those who used to feed us
When we were young — they cannot be!

THE DARKLING THRUSH

I LEANT upon a coppice gate
    When Frost was spectre-gray,
And Winter's dregs made desolate
    The weakening eye of day.
The tangled bine-stems scored the sky
    Like strings of broken lyres,
And all mankind that haunted nigh
    Had sought their household fires.

The land's sharp features seemed to be
    The Century's corpse outleant,
His crypt the cloudy canopy,
    The wind his death-lament.
The ancient pulse of germ and birth
    Was shrunken hard and dry,
And every spirit upon earth
    Seemed fervourless as I.

At once a voice arose among
    The bleak twigs overhead
In a full-hearted evensong
    Of joy illimited;
An aged thrush, frail, gaunt, and small,
    In blast-beruffled plume,
Had chosen thus to fling his soul
    Upon the growing gloom.

So little cause for carolings
    Of such ecstatic sound
Was written on terrestrial things
    Afar or nigh around,
That I could think there trembled through
    His happy good-night air
Some blessed Hope, whereof he knew
    And I was unaware.

31st December 1900.

A WASTED ILLNESS

THROUGH vaults of pain,
Enribbed and wrought with groins of ghastliness,
I passed, and garish spectres moved my brain
    To dire distress.

    And hammerings,
And quakes, and shoots, and stifling hotness, blent
With webby waxing things and waning things
    As on I went.

    'Where lies the end
To this foul way?' I asked with weakening breath.
Thereon ahead I saw a door extend —
    The door to Death.

    It loomed more clear:
'At last!' I cried. 'The all-delivering door!'
And then, I knew not how, it grew less near
    Than theretofore.

And back slid I
Along the galleries by which I came,
And tediously the day returned, and sky,
        And life — the same.

And all was well :
Old circumstance resumed its former show,
And on my head the dews of comfort fell
        As ere my woe.

I roam anew,
Scarce conscious of my late distress. . . . And yet
Those backward steps to strength I cannot view
        Without regret.

For that dire train
Of waxing shapes and waning, passed before,
And those grim chambers, must be ranged again
        To reach that door.

THE RUINED MAID

'O 'MELIA, my dear, this does everything crown !
Who could have supposed I should meet you in Town ?
And whence such fair garments, such prosperi-ty ?'—
'O didn't you know I'd been ruined ?' said she.

—'You left us in tatters, without shoes or socks,
Tired of digging potatoes, and spudding up docks;
And now you've gay bracelets and bright feathers three !'—
'Yes : that's how we dress when we're ruined,' said she.

—'At home in the barton you said "thee" and "thou",
And "thik oon", and "theäs oon", and "t'other"; but now
Your talking quite fits 'ee for high compa-ny!'—
'Some polish is gained with one's ruin,' said she.

—'Your hands were like paws then, your face blue and bleak
But now I'm bewitched by your delicate cheek,
And your little gloves fit as on any la-dy!'—
'We never do work when we're ruined,' said she.

—'You used to call home-life a hag-ridden dream,
And you'd sigh, and you'd sock; but at present you seem
To know not of megrims or melancho-ly!'—
'True. One's pretty lively when ruined,' said she.

—'I wish I had feathers, a fine sweeping gown,
And a delicate face, and could strut about Town!'—
'My dear — a raw country girl, such as you be,
Cannot quite expect that. You ain't ruined,' said she.

Westbourne Park Villas, 1866.

THE SELF-UNSEEING

Here is the ancient floor,
Footworn and hollowed and thin,
Here was the former door
Where the dead feet walked in.

She sat here in her chair,
Smiling into the fire;
He who played stood there,
Bowing it higher and higher.

Childlike, I danced in a dream;
Blessings emblazoned that day;
Everything glowed with a gleam;
Yet we were looking away!

IN TENEBRIS

I

'Percussus sum sicut foenum, et aruit cor meum.' — *Ps.* ci.

WINTERTIME nighs;
But my bereavement-pain
It cannot bring again:
Twice no one dies.

Flower-petals flee;
But, since it once hath been,
No more that severing scene
Can harrow me.

Birds faint in dread:
I shall not lose old strength
In the lone frost's black length:
Strength long since fled!

Leaves freeze to dun;
But friends can not turn cold
This season as of old
For him with none.

Tempests may scath;
But love can not make smart
Again this year his heart
Who no heart hath.

Black is night's cope;
But death will not appal
One who, past doubtings all,
Waits in unhope.

TIME'S LAUGHINGSTOCKS
AND OTHER VERSES

TIME'S LAUGHINGSTOCKS

A TRAMPWOMAN'S TRAGEDY

(182–)

I

FROM Wynyard's Gap the livelong day,
  The livelong day,
We beat afoot the northward way
  We had travelled times before.
The sun-blaze burning on our backs,
Our shoulders sticking to our packs,
By fosseway, fields, and turnpike tracks
  We skirted sad Sedge-Moor.

II

Full twenty miles we jaunted on,
  We jaunted on,—
My fancy-man, and jeering John,
  And Mother Lee, and I.
And, as the sun drew down to west,
We climbed the toilsome Poldon crest,
And saw, of landskip sights the best,
  The inn that beamed thereby.

III

For months we had padded side by side,
  Ay, side by side
Through the Great Forest, Blackmoor wide,
  And where the Parret ran.

We'd faced the gusts on Mendip ridge,
Had crossed the Yeo unhelped by bridge,
Been stung by every Marshwood midge,
    I and my fancy-man.

IV

Lone inns we loved, my man and I,
    My man and I;
'King's Stag', 'Windwhistle' high and dry,
    'The Horse' on Hintock Green,
The cosy house at Wynyard's Gap,
'The Hut' renowned on Bredy Knap,
And many another wayside tap
    Where folk might sit unseen.

V

Now as we trudged — O deadly day,
    O deadly day! —
I teased my fancy-man in play
    And wanton idleness.
I walked alongside jeering John,
I laid his hand my waist upon;
I would not bend my glances on
    My lover's dark distress.

VI

Thus Poldon top at last we won,
    At last we won,
And gained the inn at sink of sun
    Far-famed as 'Marshal's Elm'.
Beneath us figured tor and lea,
From Mendip to the western sea —
I doubt if finer sight there be
    Within this royal realm.

VII

Inside the settle all a-row —
    All four a-row
We sat, I next to John, to show
    That he had wooed and won.
And then he took me on his knee,
And swore it was his turn to be
My favoured mate, and Mother Lee
    Passed to my former one.

VIII

Then in a voice I had never heard,
    I had never heard,
My only Love to me: 'One word,
    My lady, if you please!
Whose is the child you are like to bear? —
His? After all my months o' care?'
God knows 'twas not! But, O despair!
    I nodded — still to tease.

IX

Then up he sprung, and with his knife —
    And with his knife
He let out jeering Johnny's life,
    Yes; there, at set of sun.
The slant ray through the window nigh
Gilded John's blood and glazing eye,
Ere scarcely Mother Lee and I
    Knew that the deed was done.

X

The taverns tell the gloomy tale,
    The gloomy tale,
How that at Ivel-chester jail
    My Love, my sweetheart swung;

Though stained till now by no misdeed
Save one horse ta'en in time o' need;
(Blue Jimmy stole right many a steed
        Ere his last fling he flung.)

XI

Thereaft I walked the world alone,
        Alone, alone!
On his death-day I gave my groan
        And dropt his dead-born child.
'Twas nigh the jail, beneath a tree,
None tending me; for Mother Lee
Had died at Glaston, leaving me
        Unfriended on the wild.

XII

And in the night as I lay weak,
        As I lay weak,
The leaves a-falling on my cheek,
        The red moon low declined —
The ghost of him I'd die to kiss
Rose up and said : 'Ah, tell me this!
Was the child mine, or was it his?
        Speak, that I rest may find!'

XIII

O doubt not but I told him then,
        I told him then,
That I had kept me from all men
        Since we joined lips and swore.
Whereat he smiled, and thinned away
As the wind stirred to call up day . . .
— 'Tis past! And here alone I stray
        Haunting the Western Moor.

THE HOUSE OF HOSPITALITIES

HERE we broached the Christmas barrel,
　　Pushed up the charred log-ends;
Here we sang the Christmas carol,
　　And called in friends.

Time has tired me since we met here
　　When the folk now dead were young,
Since the viands were outset here
　　And quaint songs sung.

And the worm has bored the viol
　　That used to lead the tune,
Rust eaten out the dial
　　That struck night's noon.

Now no Christmas brings in neighbours,
　　And the New Year comes unlit;
Where we sang the mole now labours,
　　And spiders knit.

Yet at midnight if here walking,
　　When the moon sheets wall and tree,
I see forms of old time talking,
　　Who smile on me.

SHUT OUT THAT MOON

CLOSE up the casement, draw the blind,
　　Shut out that stealing moon,
She wears too much the guise she wore
　　Before our lutes were strewn
With years-deep dust, and names we read
　　On a white stone were hewn.

Step not forth on the dew-dashed lawn
　　To view the Lady's Chair,
Immense Orion's glittering form,
　　The Less and Greater Bear:
Stay in; to such sights we were drawn
　　When faded ones were fair.

Brush not the bough for midnight scents
　　That come forth lingeringly,
And wake the same sweet sentiments
　　They breathed to you and me
When living seemed a laugh, and love
　　All it was said to be.

Within the common lamp-lit room
　　Prison my eyes and thought;
Let dingy details crudely loom,
　　Mechanic speech be wrought:
Too fragrant was Life's early bloom,
　　Too tart the fruit it brought!

　　1904.

THE DEAD MAN WALKING

THEY hail me as one living,
　　But don't they know
That I have died of late years,
　　Untombed although?

I am but a shape that stands here,
　　A pulseless mould,
A pale past picture, screening
　　Ashes gone cold.

Not at a minute's warning,
　　Not in a loud hour,
For me ceased Time's enchantments
　　In hall and bower.

There was no tragic transit,
    No catch of breath,
When silent seasons inched me
    On to this death. . . .

— A Troubadour-youth I rambled
    With Life for lyre,
The beats of being raging
    In me like fire.

But when I practised eyeing
    The goal of men,
It iced me, and I perished
    A little then.

When passed my friend, my kinsfolk,
    Through the Last Door,
And left me standing bleakly,
    I died yet more;

And when my Love's heart kindled
    In hate of me,
Wherefore I knew not, died I
    One more degree.

And if when I died fully
    I cannot say,
And changed into the corpse-thing
    I am today,

Yet is it that, though whiling
    The time somehow
In walking, talking, smiling,
    I live not now.

MORE LOVE LYRICS

THE CONFORMERS

YES; we'll wed, my little fay,
    And you shall write you mine,
And in a villa chastely gray
    We'll house, and sleep, and dine.
    But those night-screened, divine,
    Stolen trysts of heretofore,
We of choice ecstasies and fine
        Shall know no more.

The formal faced cohue
    Will then no more upbraid
With smiting smiles and whisperings two
    Who have thrown less loves in shade.
    We shall no more evade
    The searching light of the sun,
Our game of passion will be played,
        Our dreaming done.

We shall not go in stealth
    To rendezvous unknown,
But friends will ask me of your health,
    And you about my own.
    When we abide alone,
    No leapings each to each,
But syllables in frigid tone
        Of household speech.

When down to dust we glide
Men will not say askance,
As now : 'How all the country side
    Rings with their mad romance!'
But as they graveward glance
Remark : 'In them we lose
A worthy pair, who helped advance
    Sound parish views.'

THE END OF THE EPISODE

INDULGE no more may we
In this sweet-bitter pastime :
The love-light shines the last time
    Between you, Dear, and me.

There shall remain no trace
Of what so closely tied us,
And blank as ere love eyed us
    Will be our meeting-place.

The flowers and thymy air,
Will they now miss our coming?
The dumbles thin their humming
    To find we haunt not there?

Though fervent was our vow,
Though ruddily ran our pleasure,
Bliss has fulfilled its measure,
    And sees its sentence now.

Ache deep; but make no moans :
Smile out; but stilly suffer :
The paths of love are rougher
    Than thoroughfares of stones.

A SET OF COUNTRY SONGS

FORMER BEAUTIES

THESE market-dames, mid-aged, with lips thin-drawn,
    And tissues sere,
Are they the ones we loved in years agone,
    And courted here?

Are these the muslined pink young things to whom
    We vowed and swore
In nooks on summer Sundays by the Froom,
    Or Budmouth shore?

Do they remember those gay tunes we trod
    Clasped on the green;
Aye; trod till moonlight set on the beaten sod
    A satin sheen?

They must forget, forget! They cannot know
    What once they were,
Or memory would transfigure them, and show
    Them always fair.

PIECES OCCASIONAL AND VARIOUS

A CHURCH ROMANCE
(*Mellstock: circa 1835*)

SHE turned in the high pew, until her sight
Swept the west gallery, and caught its row
Of music-men with viol, book, and bow
Against the sinking sad tower-window light.

She turned again; and in her pride's despite
One strenuous viol's inspirer seemed to throw
A message from his string to her below,
Which said : 'I claim thee as my own forthright!'

Thus their hearts' bond began, in due time signed.
And long years thence, when Age had scared Romance,
At some old attitude of his or glance
That gallery-scene would break upon her mind,
With him as minstrel, ardent, young, and trim,
Bowing 'New Sabbath' or 'Mount Ephraim'.

SHE HEARS THE STORM

THERE was a time in former years —
　　While my roof-tree was his —
When I should have been distressed by fears
　　At such a night as this!

I should have murmured anxiously,
　　'The pricking rain strikes cold;
His road is bare of hedge or tree,
　　And he is getting old.'

But now the fitful chimney-roar,
　　The drone of Thorncombe trees,
The Froom in flood upon the moor,
　　The mud of Mellstock Leaze,

The candle slanting sooty-wick'd,
　　The thuds upon the thatch,
The eaves-drops on the window flicked,
　　The clacking garden-hatch,

And what they mean to wayfarers,
　　I scarcely heed or mind;
He has won that storm-tight roof of hers
　　Which Earth grants all her kind.

THE UNBORN

I ROSE at night, and visited
　　The Cave of the Unborn:
And crowding shapes surrounded me
For tidings of the life to be,
Who long had prayed the silent Head
　　To haste its advent morn.

Their eyes were lit with artless trust,
　　Hope thrilled their every tone;
'A scene the loveliest, is it not?
A pure delight, a beauty-spot
Where all is gentle, true and just,
　　And darkness is unknown?'

My heart was anguished for their sake,
      I could not frame a word;
And they descried my sunken face,
And seemed to read therein, and trace
The news that pity would not break,
      Nor truth leave unaverred.

And as I silently retired
      I turned and watched them still,
And they came helter-skelter out,
Driven forward like a rabble rout
Into the world they had so desired,
      By the all-immanent Will.

      1905.

THE MAN HE KILLED

'HAD he and I but met
      By some old ancient inn,
We should have sat us down to wet
      Right many a nipperkin!

'But ranged as infantry,
      And staring face to face,
I shot at him as he at me,
      And killed him in his place.

'I shot him dead because —
      Because he was my foe,
Just so : my foe of course he was;
      That's clear enough; although

'He thought he'd 'list, perhaps,
    Off-hand like — just as I —
Was out of work — had sold his traps —
    No other reason why.

    'Yes; quaint and curious war is!
        You shoot a fellow down
You'd treat if met where any bar is,
    Or help to half-a-crown.'

                1902.

SATIRES OF CIRCUMSTANCE

LYRICS AND REVERIES

THE CONVERGENCE OF THE TWAIN
(*Lines on the loss of the* Titanic)

I

In a solitude of the sea
Deep from human vanity,
And the Pride of Life that planned her, stilly couches she.

II

Steel chambers, late the pyres
Of her salamandrine fires,
Cold currents thrid, and turn to rhythmic tidal lyres.

III

Over the mirrors meant
To glass the opulent
The sea-worm crawls — grotesque, slimed, dumb, indifferent.

IV

Jewels in joy designed
To ravish the sensuous mind
Lie lightless, all their sparkles bleared and black and blind.

V

Dim moon-eyed fishes near
Gaze at the gilded gear
And query: 'What does this vaingloriousness down here?'...

VI

Well : while was fashioning
This creature of cleaving wing,
The Immanent Will that stirs and urges everything

VII

Prepared a sinister mate
For her — so gaily great —
A Shape of Ice, for the time far and dissociate.

VIII

And as the smart ship grew
In stature, grace, and hue,
In shadowy silent distance grew the Iceberg too.

IX

Alien they seemed to be :
No mortal eye could see
The intimate welding of their later history,

X

Or sign that they were bent
By paths coincident
On being anon twin halves of one august event,

XI

Till the Spinner of the Years
Said 'Now !' And each one hears,
And consummation comes, and jars two hemispheres.

'MY SPIRIT WILL NOT HAUNT THE MOUND'

MY spirit will not haunt the mound
　　Above my breast,
But travel, memory-possessed,
To where my tremulous being found
　　Life largest, best.

My phantom-footed shape will go
　　When nightfall grays
Hither and thither along the ways
I and another used to know
　　In backward days.

And there you'll find me, if a jot
　　You still should care
For me, and for my curious air;
If otherwise, then I shall not,
　　For you, be there.

IN DEATH DIVIDED

I

I SHALL rot here, with those whom in their day
　　You never knew,
And alien ones who, ere they chilled to clay,
　　Met not my view,
Will in your distant grave-place ever neighbour you.

II

No shade of pinnacle or tree or tower,
    While earth endures,
Will·fall on my mound and within the hour
    Steal on to yours;
One robin never haunt our two green covertures.

III

Some organ may resound on Sunday noons
    By where you lie,
Some other thrill the panes with other tunes
    Where moulder I;
No selfsame chords compose our common lullaby.

IV

The simply-cut memorial at my head
    Perhaps may take
A rustic form, and that above your bed
    A stately make;
No linking symbol show thereon for our tale's sake.

V

And in the monotonous moils of strained, hard-run
    Humanity,
The eternal tie which binds us twain in one
    No eye will see
Stretching across the miles that sever you from me.

    189–.

A PLAINT TO MAN

WHEN you slowly emerged from the den of Time,
And gained percipience as you grew,
And fleshed you fair out of shapeless slime,

Wherefore, O Man, did there come to you
The unhappy need of creating me —
A form like your own — for praying to?

My virtue, power, utility,
Within my maker must all abide,
Since none in myself can ever be,

One thin as a phasm on a lantern-slide
Shown forth in the dark upon some dim sheet,
And by none but its showman vivified.

'Such a forced device,' you may say, 'is meet
For easing a loaded heart at whiles:
Man needs to conceive of a mercy-seat

Somewhere above the gloomy aisles
Of this wailful world, or he could not bear
The irk no local hope beguiles.'

— But since I was framed in your first despair
The doing without me has had no play
In the minds of men when shadows scare;

And now that I dwindle day by day
Beneath the deicide eyes of seers
In a light that will not let me stay,

And tomorrow the whole of me disappears,
The truth should be told, and the fact be faced
That had best been faced in earlier years:

The fact of life with dependence placed
On the human heart's resource alone,
In brotherhood bonded close and graced

With loving-kindness fully blown,
And visioned help unsought, unknown.

    1909–10.

AT DAY-CLOSE IN NOVEMBER

THE ten hours' light is abating,
        And a late bird wings across,
Where the pines, like waltzers waiting,
        Give their black heads a toss.

Beech leaves, that yellow the noon-time,
        Float past like specks in the eye;
I set every tree in my June time,
        And now they obscure the sky.

And the children who ramble through here
        Conceive that there never has been
A time when no tall trees grew here,
        That none will in time be seen.

POEMS OF 1912–13

THE GOING

WHY did you give no hint that night
That quickly after the morrow's dawn,
And calmly, as if indifferent quite,
You would close your term here, up and be gone,
    Where I could not follow
    With wing of swallow
To gain one glimpse of you ever anon!

    Never to bid good-bye,
    Or lip me the softest call,
Or utter a wish for a word, while I
Saw morning harden upon the wall,
    Unmoved, unknowing
    That your great going
Had place that moment, and altered all.

Why do you make me leave the house
And think for a breath it is you I see
At the end of the alley of bending boughs
Where so often at dusk you used to be;
    Till in darkening dankness
    The yawning blankness
Of the perspective sickens me!

    You were she who abode
    By those red-veined rocks far West,
You were the swan-necked one who rode
Along the beetling Beeny Crest,

And, reining nigh me,
Would muse and eye me,
While Life unrolled us its very best.

Why, then, latterly did we not speak,
Did we not think of those days long dead,
And ere your vanishing strive to seek
That time's renewal? We might have said,
'In this bright spring weather
We'll visit together
Those places that once we visited.'

Well, well! All's past amend,
Unchangeable. It must go.
I seem but a dead man held on end
To sink down soon.... O you could not know
That such swift fleeing
No soul foreseeing —
Not even I — would undo me so!
December 1912.

YOUR LAST DRIVE

HERE by the moorway you returned,
And saw the borough lights ahead
That lit your face — all undiscerned
To be in a week the face of the dead,
And you told of the charm of that haloed view
That never again would beam on you.

And on your left you passed the spot
Where eight days later you were to lie,

And be spoken of as one who was not;
Beholding it with a heedless eye
As alien from you, though under its tree
You soon would halt everlastingly.

I drove not with you.... Yet had I sat
At your side that eve I should not have seen
That the countenance I was glancing at
Had a last-time look in the flickering sheen,
Nor have read the writing upon your face,
'I go hence soon to my resting-place;

'You may miss me then. But I shall not know
How many times you visit me there,
Or what your thoughts are, or if you go
There never at all. And I shall not care.
Should you censure me I shall take no heed,
And even your praises no more shall need.'

True: never you'll know. And you will not mind.
But shall I then slight you because of such?
Dear ghost, in the past did you ever find
The thought 'What profit,' move me much?
Yet abides the fact, indeed, the same, —
You are past love, praise, indifference, blame.
   December 1912.

THE WALK

You did not walk with me
Of late to the hill-top tree
  By the gated ways,
  As in earlier days;
  You were weak and lame,
  So you never came,
And I went alone, and I did not mind,
Not thinking of you as left behind.

I walked up there today
Just in the former way;
  Surveyed around
  The familiar ground
  By myself again :
  What difference, then?
Only that underlying sense
Of the look of a room on returning thence.

RAIN ON A GRAVE

Clouds spout upon her
  Their waters amain
  In ruthless disdain, —
Her who but lately
  Had shivered with pain

As at touch of dishonour
If there had lit on her
So coldly, so straightly
   Such arrows of rain :

One who to shelter
   Her delicate head
Would quicken and quicken
   Each tentative tread
If drops chanced to pelt her
   That summertime spills
   In dust-paven rills
When thunder-clouds thicken
   And birds close their bills.

Would that I lay there
   And she were housed here !
Or better, together
Were folded away there
Exposed to one weather
We both, — who would stray there
When sunny the day there,
   Or evening was clear
   At the prime of the year.

Soon will be growing
   Green blades from her mound,
And daisies be showing
   Like stars on the ground,
Till she form part of them —
Ay — the sweet heart of them,
Loved beyond measure
With a child's pleasure
   All her life's round.

Jan. 31, 1913.

'I FOUND HER OUT THERE'

I FOUND her out there
On a slope few see,
That falls westwardly
To the salt-edged air,
Where the ocean breaks
On the purple strand,
And the hurricane shakes
The solid land.

I brought her here,
And have laid her to rest
In a noiseless nest
No sea beats near.
She will never be stirred
In her loamy cell
By the waves long heard
And loved so well.

So she does not sleep
By those haunted heights
The Atlantic smites
And the blind gales sweep,
Whence she often would gaze
At Dundagel's famed head,
While the dipping blaze
Dyed her face fire-red;

And would sigh at the tale
Of sunk Lyonnesse,
As a wind-tugged tress
Flapped her cheek like a flail;

Or listen at whiles
With a thought-bound brow
To the murmuring miles
She is far from now.

Yet her shade, maybe,
Will creep underground
Till it catch the sound
Of that western sea
As it swells and sobs
Where she once domiciled,
And joy in its throbs
With the heart of a child.

WITHOUT CEREMONY

It was your way, my dear,
To vanish without a word
When callers, friends, or kin
Had left, and I hastened in
To rejoin you, as I inferred.

And when you'd a mind to career
Off anywhere — say to town —
You were all on a sudden gone
Before I had thought thereon,
Or noticed your trunks were down.

So, now that you disappear
For ever in that swift style,
Your meaning seems to me
Just as it used to be:
'Good-bye is not worth while!'

THE VOICE

WOMAN much missed, how you call to me, call to me,
Saying that now you are not as you were
When you had changed from the one who was all to me,
But as at first, when our day was fair.

Can it be you that I hear? Let me view you, then,
Standing as when I drew near to the town
Where you would wait for me: yes, as I knew you then,
Even to the original air-blue gown!

Or is it only the breeze, in its listlessness
Travelling across the wet mead to me here,
You being ever dissolved to wan wistlessness,
Heard no more again far or near?

　　　Thus I; faltering forward,
　　　Leaves around me falling,
Wind oozing thin through the thorn from norward,
　　　And the woman calling.

　　December 1912.

AFTER A JOURNEY

HERETO I come to view a voiceless ghost;
　　Whither, O whither will its whim now draw me?
Up the cliff, down, till I'm lonely, lost,
　　And the unseen waters' ejaculations awe me.
Where you will next be there's no knowing,
　　Facing round about me everywhere,
　　　　With your nut-coloured hair,
And gray eyes, and rose-flush coming and going.

Yes: I have re-entered your olden haunts at last;
> Through the years, through the dead scenes I have tracked
> > you;
What have you now found to say of our past —
> Scanned across the dark space wherein I have lacked you?
Summer gave us sweets, but autumn wrought division?
> Things were not lastly as firstly well
> > With us twain, you tell?
But all's closed now, despite Time's derision.

I see what you are doing: you are leading me on
> To the spots we knew when we haunted here together,
The waterfall, above which the mist-bow shone
> At the then fair hour in the then fair weather,
And the cave just under, with a voice still so hollow
> That it seems to call out to me from forty years ago,
> > When you were all aglow,
And not the thin ghost that I now fraily follow!

Ignorant of what there is flitting here to see,
> The waked birds preen and the seals flop lazily;
Soon you will have, Dear, to vanish from me,
> For the stars close their shutters and the dawn whitens
> > hazily.
Trust me, I mind not, though Life lours,
> The bringing me here; nay, bring me here again!
> > I am just the same as when
Our days were a joy, and our paths through flowers.

PENTARGAN BAY.

AT CASTLE BOTEREL

As I drive to the junction of lane and highway,
  And the drizzle bedrenches the waggonette,
I look behind at the fading byway,
  And see on its slope, now glistening wet,
    Distinctly yet

Myself and a girlish form benighted
  In dry March weather. We climb the road
Beside a chaise. We had just alighted
  To ease the sturdy pony's load
    When he sighed and slowed.

What we did as we climbed, and what we talked of
  Matters not much, nor to what it led, —
Something that life will not be balked of
  Without rude reason till hope is dead,
    And feeling fled.

It filled but a minute. But was there ever
  A time of such quality, since or before,
In that hill's story? To one mind never,
  Though it has been climbed, foot-swift, foot-sore,
    By thousands more.

Primaeval rocks form the road's steep border,
  And much have they faced there, first and last,
Of the transitory in Earth's long order;
  But what they record in colour and cast
    Is — that we two passed.

And to me, though Time's unflinching rigour,
  In mindless rote, has ruled from sight
The substance now, one phantom figure
  Remains on the slope, as when that night
    Saw us alight.

I look and see it there, shrinking, shrinking,
  I look back at it amid the rain
For the very last time; for my sand is sinking,
  And I shall traverse old love's domain
    Never again.

  March 1913.

THE PHANTOM HORSEWOMAN

I

QUEER are the ways of a man I know:
    He comes and stands
    In a careworn craze,
    And looks at the sands
    And the seaward haze
    With moveless hands
    And face and gaze,
    Then turns to go ...
And what does he see when he gazes so?

II

They say he sees as an instant thing
    More clear than today,
    A sweet soft scene
    That was once in play
    By that briny green;
    Yes, notes alway
    Warm, real, and keen,
    What his back years bring —
A phantom of his own figuring.

III

Of this vision of his they might say more:
        Not only there
        Does he see this sight,
        But everywhere
        In his brain — day, night,
        As if on the air
        It were drawn rose-bright —
        Yea, far from that shore
Does he carry this vision of heretofore:

IV

A ghost-girl-rider. And though, toil-tried,
        He withers daily,
        Time touches her not,
        But she still rides gaily
        In his rapt thought
        On that shagged and shaly
        Atlantic spot,
        And as when first eyed
Draws rein and sings to the swing of the tide.

    1913.

WHERE THE PICNIC WAS

        WHERE we made the fire
        In the summer time
        Of branch and briar
        On the hill to the sea,
        I slowly climb
        Through winter mire,
        And scan and trace
        The forsaken place
        Quite readily.

Now a cold wind blows,
And the grass is gray,
But the spot still shows
As a burnt circle — aye,
And stick-ends, charred,
Still strew the sward
Whereon I stand,
Last relic of the band
Who came that day!

Yes, I am here
Just as last year,
And the sea breathes brine
From its strange straight line
Up hither, the same
As when we four came.
— But two have wandered far
From this grassy rise
Into urban roar
Where no picnics are,
And one — has shut her eyes
For evermore.

MISCELLANEOUS PIECES

IN THE SERVANTS' QUARTERS

'Man, you too, aren't you, one of these rough followers of
        the criminal?
All hanging hereabout to gather how he's going to bear
Examination in the hall.' She flung disdainful glances on
The shabby figure standing at the fire with others there,
        Who warmed them by its flare.

'No indeed, my skipping maiden: I know nothing of the
        trial here,
Or criminal, if so he be. — I chanced to come this way,
And the fire shone out into the dawn, and morning airs are
        cold now;
I, too, was drawn in part by charms I see before me play,
        That I see not every day.'

'Ha, ha!' then laughed the constables who also stood to warm
        themselves,
The while another maiden scrutinised his features hard,
As the blaze threw into contrast every line and knot that
        wrinkled them,
Exclaiming, 'Why, last night when he was brought in by the
        guard,
        You were with him in the yard!'

'Nay, nay, you teasing wench, I say! You know you speak
        mistakenly.
Cannot a tired pedestrian who has legged it long and far

Here on his way from northern parts, engrossed in humble
      marketings,
Come in and rest awhile, although judicial doings are
      Afoot by morning star?'

'O, come, come!' laughed the constables. 'Why, man, you
      speak the dialect
He uses in his answers; you can hear him up the stairs.
So own it. We sha'n't hurt ye. There he's speaking now!
      His syllables
Are those you sound yourself when you are talking unawares,
      As this pretty girl declares.'

'And you shudder when his chain clinks!' she rejoined. 'O
      yes, I noticed it.
And you winced, too, when those cuffs they gave him echoed
      to us here.
They'll soon be coming down, and you may then have to
      defend yourself
Unless you hold your tongue, or go away and keep you clear
      When he's led to judgment near!'

'No! I'll be damned in hell if I know anything about the man!
No single thing about him more than everybody knows!
Must not I even warm my hands but I am charged with
      blasphemies?' . . .
— His face convulses as the morning cock that moment
      crows,
      And he droops, and turns, and goes.

'REGRET NOT ME'

REGRET not me;
Beneath the sunny tree
I lie uncaring, slumbering peacefully.

Swift as the light
I flew my faery flight;
Ecstatically I moved, and feared no night.

I did not know
That heydays fade and go,
But deemed that what was would be always so.

I skipped at morn
Between the yellowing corn,
Thinking it good and glorious to be born.

I ran at eves
Among the piled-up sheaves,
Dreaming, 'I grieve not, therefore nothing grieves.'

Now soon will come
The apple, pear, and plum,
And hinds will sing, and autumn insects hum.

Again you will fare
To cider-makings rare,
And junketings; but I shall not be there.

Yet gaily sing
Until the pewter ring
Those songs we sang when we went gipsying.

And lightly dance
Some triple-timed romance
In coupled figures, and forget mischance;

And mourn not me
Beneath the yellowing tree;
For I shall mind not, slumbering peacefully.

SEEN BY THE WAITS

THROUGH snowy woods and shady
  We went to play a tune
To the lonely manor-lady
  By the light of the Christmas moon.

We violed till, upward glancing
  To where a mirror leaned,
It showed her airily dancing,
  Deeming her movements screened;

Dancing alone in the room there,
  Thin-draped in her robe of night;
Her postures, glassed in the gloom there,
  Were a strange phantasmal sight.

She had learnt (we heard when homing)
  That her roving spouse was dead:
Why she had danced in the gloaming
  We thought, but never said.

THE WORKBOX

'SEE, here's the workbox, little wife,
  That I made of polished oak.'
He was a joiner, of village life;
  She came of borough folk.

He holds the present up to her
  As with a smile she nears
And answers to the profferer,
  ' 'Twill last all my sewing years!'

'I warrant it will. And longer too.
   'Tis a scantling that I got
Off poor John Wayward's coffin, who
   Died of they knew not what.

'The shingled pattern that seems to cease
   Against your box's rim
Continues right on in the piece
   That's underground with him.

'And while I worked it made me think
   Of timber's varied doom;
One inch where people eat and drink,
   The next inch in a tomb.

'But why do you look so white, my dear,
   And turn aside your face?
You knew not that good lad, I fear,
   Though he came from your native place?'

'How could I know that good young man,
   Though he came from my native town,
When he must have left far earlier than
   I was a woman grown?'

'Ah, no. I should have understood!
   It shocked you that I gave
To you one end of a piece of wood
   Whose other is in a grave?'

'Don't, dear, despise my intellect,
   Mere accidental things
Of that sort never have effect
   On my imaginings.'

Yet still her lips were limp and wan,
Her face still held aside,
As if she had known not only John,
But known of what he died.

SATIRES OF CIRCUMSTANCE

I
AT TEA

THE kettle descants in a cosy drone,
And the young wife looks in her husband's face,
And then at her guest's, and shows in her own
Her sense that she fills an envied place;
And the visiting lady is all abloom,
And says there was never so sweet a room.

And the happy young housewife does not know
That the woman beside her was first his choice,
Till the fates ordained it could not be so....
Betraying nothing in look or voice
The guest sits smiling and sips her tea,
And he throws her a stray glance yearningly.

II
IN CHURCH

'AND now to God the Father,' he ends,
And his voice thrills up to the topmost tiles:
Each listener chokes as he bows and bends,
And emotion pervades the crowded aisles.
Then the preacher glides to the vestry-door,
And shuts it, and thinks he is seen no more.

The door swings softly ajar meanwhile,
And a pupil of his in the Bible class,
Who adores him as one without gloss or guile,
Sees her idol stand with a satisfied smile
And re-enact at the vestry-glass
Each pulpit gesture in deft dumb-show
That had moved the congregation so.

XII

AT THE DRAPER'S

'I STOOD at the back of the shop, my dear,
    But you did not perceive me.
Well, when they deliver what you were shown
    I shall know nothing of it, believe me!'

And he coughed and coughed as she paled and said,
    'O, I didn't see you come in there —
Why couldn't you speak?' — 'Well, I didn't. I left
    That you should not notice I'd been there.

'You were viewing some lovely things. "*Soon required
    For a widow, of latest fashion*";
And I knew 'twould upset you to meet the man
    Who had to be cold and ashen

'And screwed in a box before they could dress you
    "*In the last new note in mourning*",
As they defined it. So, not to distress you,
    I left you to your adorning.'

XV

IN THE MOONLIGHT

O LONELY workman, standing there
In a dream, why do you stare and stare
At her grave, as no other grave there were?

'If your great gaunt eyes so importune
Her soul by the shine of this corpse-cold moon,
Maybe you'll raise her phantom soon!'

'Why, fool, it is what I would rather see
Than all the living folk there be;
But alas, there is no such joy for me!'

'Ah — she was one you loved, no doubt,
Through good and evil, through rain and drought,
And when she passed, all your sun went out?'

'Nay: she was the woman I did not love,
Whom all the others were ranked above,
Whom during her life I thought nothing of.'

MOMENTS OF VISION AND MISCELLANEOUS VERSES

AFTERNOON SERVICE AT MELLSTOCK

(circa 1850)

On afternoons of drowsy calm
We stood in the panelled pew,
Singing one-voiced a Tate-and-Brady psalm
To the tune of 'Cambridge New'.

We watched the elms, we watched the rooks,
The clouds upon the breeze,
Between the whiles of glancing at our books,
And swaying like the trees.

So mindless were those outpourings! —
Though I am not aware
That I have gained by subtle thought on things
Since we stood psalming there.

HEREDITY

I am the family face;
Flesh perishes, I live on,
Projecting trait and trace
Through time to times anon,
And leaping from place to place
Over oblivion.

The years-heired feature that can
In curve and voice and eye
Despise the human span

Of durance — that is I;
The eternal thing in man,
That heeds no call to die.

ON A MIDSUMMER EVE

I IDLY cut a parsley stalk,
And blew therein towards the moon;
I had not thought what ghosts would walk
With shivering footsteps to my tune.

I went, and knelt, and scooped my hand
As if to drink, into the brook,
And a faint figure seemed to stand
Above me, with the bygone look.

I lipped rough rhymes of chance, not choice,
I thought not what my words might be;
There came into my ear a voice
That turned a tenderer verse for me.

LINES

TO A MOVEMENT IN MOZART'S E-FLAT SYMPHONY

SHOW me again the time
When in the Junetide's prime
We flew by meads and mountains northerly! —
Yea, to such freshness, fairness, fulness, fineness, freeness,
Love lures life on.

Show me again the day
When from the sandy bay
We looked together upon the pestered sea! —
Yea, to such surging, swaying, sighing, swelling, shrinking,
    Love lures life on.

Show me again the hour
When by the pinnacled tower
We eyed each other and feared futurity! —
Yea, to such bodings, broodings, beatings, blanchings, bless-
      ings,
    Love lures life on.

Show me again just this:
The moment of that kiss
Away from the prancing folk, by the strawberry-tree! —
Yea, to such rashness, ratheness, rareness, ripeness, richness,
    Love lures life on.

   Begun November 1898.

'SOMETHING TAPPED'

SOMETHING tapped on the pane of my room
   When there was never a trace
Of wind or rain, and I saw in the gloom
   My weary Beloved's face.

O I am tired of waiting,' she said,
   'Night, morn, noon, afternoon;
So cold it is in my lonely bed,
   And I thought you would join me soon!'

I rose and neared the window-glass,
 But vanished thence had she :
Only a pallid moth, alas,
 Tapped at the pane for me.

 August 1913.

THE ANNOUNCEMENT

They came, the brothers, and took two chairs
 In their usual quiet way;
And for a time we did not think
 They had much to say.

And they began and talked awhile
 Of ordinary things,
Till spread that silence in the room
 A pent thought brings.

And then they said : 'The end has come.
 Yes : it has come at last.'
And we looked down, and knew that day
 A spirit had passed.

THE OXEN

CHRISTMAS EVE, and twelve of the clock.
 'Now they are all on their knees,'
An elder said as we sat in a flock
 By the embers in hearthside ease.

We pictured the meek mild creatures where
    They dwelt in their strawy pen,
Nor did it occur to one of us there
    To doubt they were kneeling then.

So fair a fancy few would weave
    In these years! Yet, I feel,
If someone said on Christmas Eve,
    'Come; see the oxen kneel

'In the lonely barton by yonder coomb
    Our childhood used to know,'
I should go with him in the gloom,
    Hoping it might be so.

    1915.

IN HER PRECINCTS

HER house looked cold from the foggy lea,
And the square of each window a dull black blur
    Where showed no stir:
Yes, her gloom within at the lack of me
Seemed matching mine at the lack of her.

The black squares grew to be squares of light
As the eveshade swathed the house and lawn,
    And viols gave tone;
There was glee within. And I found that night
The gloom of severance mine alone.

KINGSTON-MAURWARD PARK.

TRANSFORMATIONS

PORTION of this yew
Is a man my grandsire knew,
Bosomed here at its foot:
This branch may be his wife,
A ruddy human life
Now turned to a green shoot.

These grasses must be made
Of her who often prayed,
Last century, for repose;
And the fair girl long ago
Whom I often tried to know
May be entering this rose.

So, they are not underground,
But as nerves and veins abound
In the growths of upper air,
And they feel the sun and rain,
And the energy again
That made them what they were!

GREAT THINGS

SWEET cyder is a great thing,
    A great thing to me,
Spinning down to Weymouth town
    By Ridgway thirstily,
And maid and mistress summoning
    Who tend the hostelry:
O cyder is a great thing,
    A great thing to me!

The dance it is a great thing,
  A great thing to me,
With candles lit and partners fit
  For night-long revelry;
And going home when day-dawning
  Peeps pale upon the lea :
O dancing is a great thing,
  A great thing to me !

Love is, yea, a great thing,
  ˌA great thing to me,
When, having drawn across the lawn
  In darkness silently,
A figure flits like one a-wing
  Out from the nearest tree :
O love is, yes, a great thing,
  A great thing to me !

Will these be always great things,
  Great things to me? . . .
Let it befall that One will call,
  'Soul, I have need of thee :'
What then? Joy-jaunts, impassioned flings,
  Love, and its ecstasy,
Will always have been great things,
  Great things to me !

OLD FURNITURE

I KNOW not how it may be with others
  Who sit amid relics of householdry
That date from the days of their mothers' mothers,
  But well I know how it is with me
        Continually.

I see the hands of the generations
        That owned each shiny familiar thing
In play on its knobs and indentations,
        And with its ancient fashioning
            Still dallying:

Hands behind hands, growing paler and paler,
        As in a mirror a candle-flame
Shows images of itself, each frailer
        As it recedes, though the eye may frame
            Its shape the same.

On the clock's dull dial a foggy finger,
        Moving to set the minutes right
With tentative touches that lift and linger
        In the wont of a moth on a summer night,
            Creeps to my sight.

On this old viol, too, fingers are dancing —
        As whilom — just over the strings by the nut,
The tip of a bow receding, advancing
        In airy quivers, as if it would cut
            The plaintive gut.

And I see a face by that box for tinder,
        Glowing forth in fits from the dark,
And fading again, as the linten cinder
        Kindles to red at the flinty spark,
            Or goes out stark.

Well, well. It is best to be up and doing,
        The world has no use for one today
Who eyes things thus — no aim pursuing!
        He should not continue in this stay,
            But sink away.

LOGS ON THE HEARTH

A MEMORY OF A SISTER

THE fire advances along the log
  Of the tree we felled,
Which bloomed and bore striped apples by the peck
  Till its last hour of bearing knelled.

The fork that first my hand would reach
  And then my foot
In climbings upward inch by inch, lies now
  Sawn, sapless, darkening with soot.

Where the bark chars is where, one year,
  It was pruned, and bled —
Then overgrew the wound. But now, at last,
  Its growings all have stagnated.

My fellow-climber rises dim
  From her chilly grave —
Just as she was, her foot near mine on the bending limb,
  Laughing, her young brown hand awave.

December 1915.

DURING WIND AND RAIN

THEY sing their dearest songs —
He, she, all of them — yea,
Treble and tenor and bass,
  And one to play;
With the candles mooning each face....
  Ah, no; the years O!
How the sick leaves reel down in throngs!

They clear the creeping moss —
Elders and juniors — aye,
Making the pathways neat
   And the garden gay;
And they build a shady seat. . . .
   Ah, no; the years, the years;
See, the white storm-birds wing across!

They are blithely breakfasting all —
Men and maidens — yea,
Under the summer tree,
   With a glimpse of the bay,
While pet fowl come to the knee. . . .
   Ah, no; the years O!
And the rotten rose is ript from the wall.

They change to a high new house,
He, she, all of them — aye,
Clocks and carpets and chairs
   On the lawn all day,
And brightest things that are theirs. . . .
   Ah, no; the years, the years;
Down their carved names the rain-drop ploughs.

PAYING CALLS

I went by footpath and by stile
   Beyond where bustle ends,
Strayed here a mile and there a mile
   And called upon some friends.

On certain ones I had not seen
   For years past did I call,
And then on others who had been
   The oldest friends of all.

It was the time of midsummer
　　When they had used to roam;
But now, though tempting was the air,
　　I found them all at home.

I spoke to one and other of them
　　By mound and stone and tree
Of things we had done ere days were dim,
　　But they spoke not to me.

'WHO'S IN THE NEXT ROOM?'

'Who's in the next room? — who?
　　I seemed to see
Somebody in the dawning passing through,
　　Unknown to me.'
'Nay: you saw nought. He passed invisibly.'

'Who's in the next room? — who?
　　I seem to hear
Somebody muttering firm in a language new
　　That chills the ear.'
'No: you catch not his tongue who has entered there.'

'Who's in the next room? — who?
　　I seem to feel
His breath like a clammy draught, as if it drew
　　From the Polar Wheel.'
'No: none who breathes at all does the door conceal.'

'Who's in the next room? — who?
　　A figure wan
With a message to one in there of something due?
　　Shall I know him anon?'
'Yea he; and he brought such; and you'll know him anon.'

MIDNIGHT ON THE GREAT WESTERN

In the third-class seat sat the journeying boy,
      And the roof-lamp's oily flame
Played down on his listless form and face,
Bewrapt past knowing to what he was going,
      Or whence he came.

In the band of his hat the journeying boy
      Had a ticket stuck; and a string
Around his neck bore the key of his box,
That twinkled gleams of the lamp's sad beams
      Like a living thing.

What past can be yours, O journeying boy
      Towards a world unknown,
Who calmly, as if incurious quite
On all at stake, can undertake
      This plunge alone?

Knows your soul a sphere, O journeying boy,
      Our rude realms far above,
Whence with spacious vision you mark and mete
This region of sin that you find you in,
      But are not of?

POEMS OF WAR AND PATRIOTISM

IN TIME OF 'THE BREAKING OF NATIONS'

I

Only a man harrowing clods
   In a slow silent walk
With an old horse that stumbles and nods
   Half asleep as they stalk.

II

Only thin smoke without flame
   From the heaps of couch-grass;
Yet this will go onward the same
   Though Dynasties pass.

III

Yonder a maid and her wight
   Come whispering by:
War's annals will cloud into night
   Ere their story die.

1915.

'I LOOKED UP FROM MY WRITING'

I looked up from my writing,
   And gave a start to see,
As if rapt in my inditing,
   The moon's full gaze on me.

Her meditative misty head
　　Was spectral in its air,
And I involuntarily said,
　　'What are you doing there?'

'Oh, I've been scanning pond and hole
　　And waterway hereabout
For the body of one with a sunken soul
　　Who has put his life-light out.

'Did you hear his frenzied tattle?
　　It was sorrow for his son
Who is slain in brutish battle,
　　Though he has injured none.

'And now I am curious to look
　　Into the blinkered mind
Of one who wants to write a book
　　In a world of such a kind.'

Her temper overwrought me,
　　And I edged to shun her view,
For I felt assured she thought me
　　One who should drown him too.

FINALE

AFTERWARDS

WHEN the Present has latched its postern behind my tremu-
lous stay,
   And the May month flaps its glad green leaves like wings,
Delicate-filmed as new-spun silk, will the neighbours say,
   'He was a man who used to notice such things'?

If it be in the dusk when, like an eyelid's soundless blink,
   The dewfall-hawk comes crossing the shades to alight
Upon the wind-warped upland thorn, a gazer may think,
   'To him this must have been a familiar sight.'

If I pass during some nocturnal blackness, mothy and warm,
   When the hedgehog travels furtively over the lawn,
One may say, 'He strove that such innocent creatures should
      come to no harm,
   But he could do little for them; and now he is gone.'

If, when hearing that I have been stilled at last, they stand
      at the door,
   Watching the full-starred heavens that winter sees,
Will this thought rise on those who will meet my face no
      more,
   'He was one who had an eye for such mysteries'?

And will any say when my bell of quittance is heard in the
      gloom,
   And a crossing breeze cuts a pause in its outrollings,
Till they rise again, as they were a new bell's boom,
   'He hears it not now, but used to notice such things'?

LATE LYRICS AND EARLIER

AT THE RAILWAY STATION, UPWAY

'THERE is not much that I can do,
    For I've no money that's quite my own!'
Spoke up the pitying child —
A little boy with a violin
At the station before the train came in,—
'But I can play my fiddle to you,
And a nice one 'tis, and good in tone!'

The man in the handcuffs smiled;
The constable looked, and he smiled, too,
    As the fiddle began to twang;
And the man in the handcuffs suddenly sang
        With grimful glee:
        'This life so free
        Is the thing for me!'
And the constable smiled, and said no word,
As if unconscious of what he heard;
And so they went on till the train came in —
The convict, and boy with the violin.

AN AUTUMN RAIN-SCENE

THERE trudges one to a merry-making
        With a sturdy swing,
    On whom the rain comes down.

To fetch the saving medicament
        Is another bent,
    On whom the rain comes down.

One slowly drives his herd to the stall
        Ere ill befall,
    On whom the rain comes down.

This bears his missives of life and death
        With quickening breath,
    On whom the rain comes down.

One watches for signals of wreck or war
        From the hill afar,
    On whom the rain comes down.

No care if he gain a shelter or none,
        Unhired moves one,
    On whom the rain comes down.

And another knows nought of its chilling fall
        Upon him at all,
    On whom the rain comes down.

                October 1904.

VOICES FROM THINGS GROWING IN A CHURCHYARD

THESE flowers are I, poor Fanny Hurd,
        Sir or Madam,
A little girl here sepultured.
Once I flit-fluttered like a bird

Above the grass, as now I wave
In daisy shapes above my grave,
> All day cheerily,
> All night eerily!

— I am one Bachelor Bowring, 'Gent,'
> Sir or Madam:
In shingled oak my bones were pent;
Hence more than a hundred years I spent
In my feat of change from a coffin-thrall
To a dancer in green as leaves on a wall,
> All day cheerily,
> All night eerily!

— I, these berries of juice and gloss,
> Sir or Madam,
Am clean forgotten as Thomas Voss;
Thin-urned, I have burrowed away from the moss
That covers my sod, and have entered this yew,
And turned to clusters ruddy of view,
> All day cheerily,
> All night eerily!

— The Lady Gertrude, proud, high-bred,
> Sir or Madam,
Am I — this laurel that shades your head;
Into its veins I have stilly sped,
And made them of me; and my leaves now shine,
As did my satins superfine,
> All day cheerily,
> All night eerily!

— I, who as innocent withwind climb,
> Sir or Madam,
Am one Eve Greensleeves, in olden time
Kissed by men from many a clime,

Beneath sun, stars, in blaze, in breeze,
As now by glowworms and by bees,
        All day cheerily,
        All night eerily!¹

— I'm old Squire Audeley Grey, who grew,
        Sir or Madam,
Aweary of life, and in scorn withdrew;
Till anon I clambered up anew
As ivy-green, when my ache was stayed,
And in that attire I have longtime gayed,
        All day cheerily,
        All night eerily!

— And so these maskers breathe to each
        Sir or Madam
Who lingers there, and their lively speech
Affords an interpreter much to teach,
As their murmurous accents seem to come
Thence hitheraround in a radiant hum,
        All day cheerily,
        All night eerily!

IN THE SMALL HOURS

I LAY in my bed and fiddled
    With a dreamland viol and bow,
And the tunes flew back to my fingers
    I had melodied years ago

¹ It was said her real name was Eve Trevillian or Trevelyan; and
that she was the handsome mother of two or three illegitimate
children, *circa* 1784-95.

It was two or three in the morning
   When I fancy-fiddled so
Long reels and country-dances,
   And hornpipes swift and slow.

And soon anon came crossing
   The chamber in the gray
Figures of jigging fieldfolk —
   Saviours of corn and hay —
To the air of 'Haste to the Wedding',
   As after a wedding-day;
Yea, up and down the middle
   In windless whirls went they!

There danced the bride and bridegroom,
   And couples in a train,
Gay partners time and travail
   Had longwhiles stilled amain! ...
It seemed a thing for weeping
   To find, at slumber's wane
And morning's sly increeping,
   That Now, not Then, held reign.

ON ONE WHO LIVED AND DIED WHERE HE WAS BORN

When a night in November
   Blew forth its bleared airs
An infant descended
   His birth-chamber stairs
   For the very first time,
   At the still, midnight chime;

All unapprehended
  His mission, his aim.—
Thus, first, one November,
An infant descended
    The stairs.

On a night in November
  Of weariful cares,
A frail aged figure
  Ascended those stairs
  For the very last time :
  All gone his life's prime,
All vanished his vigour,
  And fine, forceful frame :
Thus, last, one November
Ascended that figure
    Upstairs.

On those nights in November —
  Apart eighty years —
The babe and the bent one
  Who traversed those stairs
  From the early first time
  To the last feeble climb —
That fresh and that spent one —
  Were even the same :
Yea, who passed in November
As infant, as bent one,
    Those stairs.

Wise child of November !
  From birth to blanched hairs
Descending, ascending,
  Wealth-wantless, those stairs;
  Who saw quick in time
  As a vain pantomime

Life's tending, its ending,
  The worth of its fame.
Wise child of November,
Descending, ascending
  Those stairs!

THE WHITEWASHED WALL

WHY does she turn in that shy soft way
  Whenever she stirs the fire,
And kiss to the chimney-corner wall,
  As if entranced to admire
Its whitewashed bareness more than the sight
  Of a rose in richest green?
I have known her long, but this raptured rite
  I never before have seen.

— Well, once when her son cast his shadow there,
  A friend took a pencil and drew him
Upon that flame-lit wall. And the lines
  Had a lifelike semblance to him.
And there long stayed his familiar look;
  But one day, ere she knew,
The whitener came to cleanse the nook,
  And covered the face from view.

'Yes,' he said: 'My brush goes on with a rush,
  And the draught is buried under;
When you have to whiten old cots and brighten,
  What else can you do, I wonder?'
But she knows he's there. And when she yearns
  For him, deep in the labouring night,
She sees him as close at hand, and turns
  To him under his sheet of white.

HUMAN SHOWS,
FAR PHANTASIES,
SONGS, AND TRIFLES

THE PROSPECT

THE twigs of the birch imprint the December sky
   Like branching veins upon a thin old hand;
I think of summer-time, yes, of last July,
      When she was beneath them, greeting a gathered band
         Of the urban and bland.

Iced airs wheeze through the skeletoned hedge from the
         north,
   With steady snores, and a numbing that threatens snow,
And skaters pass; and merry boys go forth
      To look for slides. But well, well do I know
         Whither I would go!

   December 1912.

WHEN OATS WERE REAPED

THAT day when oats were reaped, and wheat was ripe, and
         barley ripening,
      The road-dust hot, and the bleaching grasses dry,
         I walked along and said,
While looking just ahead to where some silent people lie:

'I wounded one who's there, and now know well I wounded
         her;
      But, ah, she does not know that she wounded me!'
         And not an air stirred,
Nor a bill of any bird; and no response accorded she.

   August 1913.

'NOT ONLY I'

NOT only I
Am doomed awhile to lie
In this close bin with earthen sides;
But the things I thought, and the songs I sang,
And the hopes I had, and the passioned pang
For people I knew
Who passed before me,
Whose memory barely abides;
And the visions I drew
That daily upbore me!

And the joyous springs and summers,
And the jaunts with blithe newcomers,
And my plans and appearances; drives and rides
That fanned my face to a lively red;
And the grays and blues
Of the far-off views,
That nobody else discerned outspread;
And little achievements for blame or praise;
Things left undone; things left unsaid;
In brief, my days!

Compressed here in six feet by two,
In secrecy
To lie with me
Till the Call shall be,
Are all these things I knew,
Which cannot be handed on;
Strange happenings quite unrecorded,
Lost to the world and disregarded,
That only thinks: 'Here moulders till Doom's-dawn
A woman's skeleton.'

SONG TO AN OLD BURDEN

THE feet have left the wormholed flooring,
    That danced to the ancient air,
    The fiddler, all-ignoring,
Sleeps by the gray-grassed 'cello player:
Shall I then foot around around around,
    As once I footed there!

The voice is heard in the room no longer
    That trilled, none sweetlier,
    To gentle stops or stronger,
Where now the dust-draped cobwebs stir:
Shall I then sing again again again,
    As once I sang with her!

The eyes that beamed out rapid brightness
    Have longtime found their close,
    The cheeks have wanned to whiteness
That used to sort with summer rose:
Shall I then joy anew anew anew,
    As once I joyed in those!

O what's to me this tedious Maying,
    What's to me this June?
    O why should viols be playing
To catch and reel and rigadoon?
Shall I sing, dance around around around,
    When phantoms call the tune!

WINTER WORDS IN
VARIOUS MOODS
AND METRES

'I AM THE ONE'

I AM the one whom ringdoves see
     Through chinks in boughs
     When they do not rouse
     In sudden dread,
But stay on cooing, as if they said:
     'Oh; it's only he.'

I am the passer when up-eared hares,
     Stirred as they eat
     The new-sprung wheat,
     Their munch resume
As if they thought: 'He is one for whom
     Nobody cares.'

Wet-eyed mourners glance at me
     As in train they pass
     Along the grass
     To a hollowed spot,
And think: 'No matter; he quizzes not
     Our misery.'

I hear above: 'We stars must lend
     No fierce regard
     To his gaze, so hard
     Bent on us thus,—
Must scathe him not. He is one with us
     Beginning and end.'

WE FIELD-WOMEN

HOW it rained
When we worked at Flintcomb-Ash,
And could not stand upon the hill
Trimming swedes for the slicing-mill.
The wet washed through us — plash, plash, plash:
How it rained!

How it snowed
When we crossed from Flintcomb-Ash
To the Great Barn for drawing reed,
Since we could nowise chop a swede.—
Flakes in each doorway and casement-sash:
How it snowed!

How it shone
When we went from Flintcomb-Ash
To start at dairywork once more
In the laughing meads, with cows three-score,
And pails, and songs, and love — too rash:
How it shone!

THE SECOND VISIT

CLACK, clack, clack, went the mill-wheel as I came,
And she was on the bridge with the thin hand-rail,
And the miller at the door, and the ducks at mill-tail;
I come again years after, and all there seems the same.

And so indeed it is: the apple-tree'd old house,
And the deep mill-pond, and the wet wheel clacking,
And a woman on the bridge, and white ducks quacking,
And the miller at the door, powdered pale from boots to
   brows.

But it's not the same miller whom long ago I knew,
Nor are they the same apples, nor the same drops that dash
Over the wet wheel, nor the ducks below that splash,
Nor the woman who to fond plaints replied, 'You know I
    do!'

THE BOY'S DREAM

PROVINCIAL town-boy he, — frail, lame,
His face a waning lily-white,
A court the home of his wry, wrenched frame,
Where noontide shed no warmth or light.

Over his temples — flat and wan,
Where bluest veins were patterned keen,
The skin appeared so thinly drawn
The skull beneath was almost seen.

Always a wishful, absent look
Expressed it in his face and eye;
At the strong shape this longing took
One guessed what wish must underlie.

But no. That wish was not for strength,
For other boys' agility,
To race with ease the field's far length,
Now hopped across so painfully.

He minded not his lameness much,
To shine at feats he did not long,
Nor to be best at goal and touch,
Nor at assaults to stand up strong.

But sometimes he would let be known
What the wish was :— to have, next spring,
A real green linnet — his very own —
Like that one he had late heard sing.

And as he breathed the cherished dream
To those whose secrecy was sworn,
His face was beautified by the theme,
And wore the radiance of the morn.

PROUD SONGSTERS

THE thrushes sing as the sun is going,
And the finches whistle in ones and pairs,
And as it gets dark loud nightingales
      In bushes
Pipe, as they can when April wears,
   As if all Time were theirs.

These are brand new birds of twelve-months' growing,
Which a year ago, or less than twain,
No finches were, nor nightingales,
      Nor thrushes,
But only particles of grain,
   And earth, and air, and rain.

LIDDELL AND SCOTT
ON THE COMPLETION OF THEIR LEXICON

*(Written after the death of Liddell in 1898. Scott had died
some ten years earlier.)*

'WELL, though it seems
Beyond our dreams,'
Said Liddell to Scott,

'We've really got
To the very end,
All inked and penned
Blotless and fair
Without turning a hair,
This sultry summer day, A.D.
Eighteen hundred and forty-three.

'I've often, I own,
Belched many a moan
At undertaking it,
And dreamt forsaking it.
— Yes, on to Pi,
When the end loomed nigh,

And friends said: "You've as good as done,"
I almost wished we'd not begun.
Even now, if people only knew
My sinkings, as we slowly drew
Along through Kappa, Lambda, Mu,
They'd be concerned at my misgiving,
And how I mused on a College living
      Right down to Sigma,
      But feared a stigma
If I succumbed, and left old Donnegan
For weary freshmen's eyes to con again:
And how I often, often wondered
What could have led me to have blundered
So far away from sound theology
To dialects and etymology;
Words, accents not to be breathed by men
Of any country ever again!'

'My heart most failed,
Indeed, quite quailed,'
Said Scott to Liddell,

'Long ere the middle! ...
'Twas one wet dawn
When, slippers on,
And a cold in the head anew,
Gazing at Delta
I turned and felt a
Wish for bed anew,
And to let supersedings
Of Passow's readings
In dialects go.
"That German has read
More than we!" I said;
Yea, several times did I feel so! ...

'O that first morning, smiling bland,
With sheets of foolscap, quills in hand,
To write ἀάατος and ἀαγής,
Followed by fifteen hundred pages,
    What nerve was ours
    So to back our powers,
Assured that we should reach ὠώδης
While there was breath left in our bodies!'

Liddell replied: 'Well, that's past now;
The job's done, thank God, anyhow.'
    'And yet it's not,'
    Considered Scott,
    'For we've to get
    Subscribers yet
    We must remember;
    Yes; by September.'

'O Lord; dismiss that. We'll succeed.
Dinner is my immediate need.
I feel as hollow as a fiddle,
Working so many hours,' said Liddell.

APPENDIX

HARDY five times introduced individual volumes of his poetry with prefaces, and since these prefaces indicate Hardy's view of his own poems it was felt that the reader of this anthology should have them conveniently available for reference. It is interesting to note that the first three prefaces are much concerned to fend off the suggestion that the views expressed, and the incidents described, are personal to the author; *Wessex Poems* are 'in a large degree dramatic or personative in conception ... even where they are not obviously so'; *Poems of the Past and the Present* contain 'much [that] is dramatic or impersonative even where not explicitly so'; *Time's Laughingstocks* 'are to be regarded, in the main, as dramatic monologues by different characters'.

These different characters had, nevertheless, a way of bearing a common resemblance to their author, and both reviewers and the public continued to make the untroubled assumption that a poem by Thomas Hardy was an utterance by and on behalf of Thomas Hardy, whose general view of life became increasingly well-known through his works. Accordingly, in the last two prefaces, Hardy is mainly concerned to combat the general view of himself as a 'pessimist'. How successfully he combated it, how cogent were the arguments he was able to bring up, the reader will decide for himself.

J. W.

WESSEX POEMS
AND OTHER VERSES

Preface

OF the miscellaneous collection of verse that follows, only four pieces have been published, though many were written long ago, and others partly written. In some few cases the verses were turned into prose and printed as such, it having been unanticipated at that time that they might see the light.

Whenever an ancient and legitimate word of the district, for which there was no equivalent in received English, suggested itself as the most natural, nearest, and often only expression of a thought, it has been made use of, on what seemed good grounds.

The pieces are in a large degree dramatic or personative in conception; and this even where they are not obviously so.

The dates attached to some of the poems do not apply to the rough sketches given in illustration,[1] which have been recently made, and, as may be surmised, are inserted for personal and local reasons rather than for their intrinsic qualities.

T. H.

September 1898.

POEMS OF
THE PAST AND THE PRESENT

Preface

HEREWITH I tender my thanks to the editors and proprietors of *The Times*, the *Morning Post*, the *Daily Chronicle*, the *Westminster Gazette*, *Literature*, the

[1] The early editions were illustrated by the writer.

Graphic, Cornhill, Sphere, and other papers, for permission to reprint from their pages such of the following pieces of verse as have already been published.

Of the subject-matter of this volume — even that which is in other than narrative form — much is dramatic or impersonative even where not explicitly so. Moreover, that portion which may be regarded as individual comprises a series of feelings and fancies written down in widely differing moods and circumstances, and at various dates. It will probably be found, therefore, to possess little cohesion of thought or harmony of colouring. I do not greatly regret this. Unadjusted impressions have their value, and the road to a true philosophy of life seems to lie in humbly recording diverse readings of its phenomena as they are forced upon us by chance and change.

T. H.

August 1901.

TIME'S LAUGHINGSTOCKS

PREFACE

IN collecting the following poems I have to thank the editors and proprietors of the periodicals in which certain of them have appeared for permission to reclaim them.

Now that the miscellany is brought together, some lack of concord in pieces written at widely severed dates, and in contrasting moods and circumstances, will be obvious enough. This I cannot help, but the sense of disconnection, particularly in respect of those lyrics penned in the first person, will be immaterial when it is borne in mind that they are to be regarded, in the main, as dramatic monologues by different characters.

As a whole they will, I hope, take the reader forward,

even if not far, rather than backward. I should add that some lines in the early-dated poems have been rewritten, though they have been left substantially unchanged.

                                                              T. H.
September 1909.

LATE LYRICS AND EARLIER

APOLOGY

ABOUT half the verses that follow were written quite lately. The rest are older, having been held over in MS. when past volumes were published, on considering that these would contain a sufficient number of pages to offer readers at one time, more especially during the distractions of the war. The unusually far back poems to be found there are, however, but some that were overlooked in gathering previous collections. A freshness in them, now unattainable, seemed to make up for their inexperience and to justify their inclusion. A few are dated; the dates of others are not discoverable.

The launching of a volume of this kind in neo-Georgian days by one who began writing in mid-Victorian, and has published nothing to speak of for some years, may seem to call for a few words of excuse or explanation. Whether or no, readers may feel assured that a new book is submitted to them with great hesitation at so belated a date. Insistent practical reasons, however, among which were requests from some illustrious men of letters who are in sympathy with my productions, the accident that several of the poems have already seen the light, and that dozens of them have been lying about for years, compelled the course adopted, in spite of the natural disinclination of a writer whose works have been so frequently regarded askance by a pragmatic section here and there, to draw attention to them once more.

I do not know that it is necessary to say much on the contents of the book, even in deference to suggestions that will be mentioned presently. I believe that those readers who care for my poems at all — readers to whom no passport is required — will care for this new instalment of them, perhaps the last, as much as for any that have preceded them. Moreover, in the eyes of a less friendly class the pieces, though a very mixed collection indeed, contain, so far as I am able to see, little or nothing in technic or teaching that can be considered a Star-Chamber matter, or so much as agitating to a ladies' school; even though, to use Wordsworth's observation in his Preface to *Lyrical Ballads*, such readers may suppose 'that by the act of writing in verse an author makes a formal engagement that he will gratify certain known habits of association : that he not only thus apprises the reader that certain classes of ideas and expressions will be found in his book, but that others will be carefully excluded'.

It is true, nevertheless, that some grave, positive, stark, delineations are interspersed among those of the passive, lighter, and traditional sort presumably nearer to stereotyped tastes. For — while I am quite aware that a thinker is not expected, and, indeed, is scarcely allowed, now more than heretofore, to state all that crosses his mind concerning existence in this universe, in his attempts to explain or excuse the presence of evil and the incongruity of penalising the irresponsible — it must be obvious to open intelligences that, without denying the beauty and faithful service of certain venerable cults, such disallowance of 'obstinate questionings' and 'blank misgivings' tends to a paralysed intellectual stalemate. Heine observed nearly a hundred years ago that the soul has her eternal rights; that she will not be darkened by statutes, nor lullabied by the music of bells. And what is today, in allusions to the present author's pages, alleged to be 'pessimism' is, in truth, only such 'questionings' in the exploration of reality, and is the first step towards the soul's betterment, and the body's also.

If I may be forgiven for quoting my own old words, let me repeat what I printed in this relation more than twenty years ago, and wrote much earlier, in a poem entitled 'In Tenebris':

If way to the Better there be, it exacts a full look at the Worst:

that is to say, by the exploration of reality, and its frank recognition stage by stage along the survey, with an eye to the best consummation possible: briefly, evolutionary meliorism. But it is called pessimism nevertheless; under which word, expressed with condemnatory emphasis, it is regarded by many as some pernicious new thing (though so old as to underlie the Gospel scheme, and even to permeate the Greek drama); and the subject is charitably left to decent silence, as if further comment were needless.

Happily there are some who feel such Levitical passing-by to be, alas, by no means a permanent dismissal of the matter; that comment on where the world stands is very much the reverse of needless in these disordered years of our prematurely afflicted century: that amendment and not madness lies that way. And looking down the future these few hold fast to the same: that whether the human and kindred animal races survive till the exhaustion or destruction of the globe, or whether these races perish and are succeeded by others before that conclusion comes, pain to all upon it, tongued or dumb, shall be kept down to a minimum by loving-kindness, operating through scientific knowledge, and actuated by the modicum of free will conjecturally possessed by organic life when the mighty necessitating forces — unconscious or other — that have 'the balancings of the clouds', happen to be in equilibrium, which may or may not be often.

To conclude this question I may add that the argument of the so-called optimists is neatly summarised in a stern pronouncement against me by my friend Mr. Frederic Harrison in a late essay of his, in the words: 'This view of life is not mine.' The solemn declaration does not seem to me to be so annihilating to the said 'view' (really a series of fugitive impressions which I have never tried to co-ordinate) as is complacently assumed. Surely it embodies a too human fallacy quite familiar in logic. Next, a knowing reviewer, apparently a Roman Catholic young man, speaks, with some rather gross instances of the *suggestio falsi* in his whole article, of 'Mr. Hardy refusing consolation', the 'dark gravity of his ideas', and so on. When a Positivist and a Romanist agree there must be something wonderful in it, which should make a poet sit up. But ... O that 'twere possible!

I would not have alluded in this place or anywhere else to such casual personal criticisms — for casual and unreflecting they must be — but for the satisfaction of two or three friends in whose opinion a short answer was deemed desirable, on account of the continual repetition of these criticisms, or more precisely, quizzings. After all, the serious and truly literary inquiry in this connection is: Should a shaper of such stuff as dreams are made on disregard considerations of what is customary and expected, and apply himself to the real function of poetry, the application of ideas to life (in Matthew Arnold's familiar phrase)? This bears more particularly on what has been called the 'philosophy' of these poems — usually reproved as 'queer'. Whoever the author may be that undertakes such application of ideas in this 'philosophic' direction — where it is specially required — glacial judgments must inevitably fall upon him amid opinion whose arbiters largely decry individuality, to whom *ideas* are oddities to smile at, who are moved by a yearning the reverse of that of the Athenian inquirers on Mars Hill; and stiffen their features not only at sound of a new thing, but at a restatement of old things in new terms. Hence should anything of this sort in the following adumbrations seem 'queer' — should any of them seem to good Panglossians to embody strange and disrespectful conceptions of this best of all possible worlds, I apologise: but cannot help it.

Such divergences, which, though piquant for the nonce, it would be affectation to say are not saddening and discouraging likewise, may, to be sure, arise sometimes from superficial aspect only, writer and reader seeing the same thing at different angles. But in palpable cases of divergence they arise, as already said, whenever a serious effort is made towards that which the authority I have cited — who would now be called old-fashioned, possibly even parochial — affirmed to be what no good critic could deny as the poet's province, the application of ideas to life. One might shrewdly guess, by the by, that in such recommendation the famous writer may have overlooked the cold-shouldering results upon an enthusiastic disciple that would be pretty certain to follow his putting the high aim in practice, and have forgotten the disconcerting experience of Gil Blas with the Archbishop.

To add a few more words to what has already taken up too many, there is a contingency liable to miscellanies of verse that I have never seen mentioned, so far as I can remember; I mean the chance little shocks that may be caused over a book of various character like the present and its predecessors by the juxtaposition of unrelated, even discordant, effusions; poems perhaps years apart in the making, yet facing each other. An odd result of this has been that dramatic anecdotes of a satirical and humorous intention following verse in graver voice, have been read as misfires because they raise the smile that they were intended to raise, the journalist, deaf to the sudden change of key, being unconscious that he is laughing with the author and not at him. I admit that I did not foresee such contingencies as I ought to have done, and that people might not perceive when the tone altered. But the difficulties of arranging the themes in a graduated kinship of moods would have been so great that irrelation was almost unavoidable with efforts so diverse. I must trust for right note-catching to those finely-touched spirits who can divine without half a whisper, whose intuitiveness is proof against all the accidents of inconsequence. In respect of the less alert, however, should any one's train of thought be thrown out of gear by a consecutive piping of vocal reeds in jarring tonics, without a semiquaver's rest between, and be led thereby to miss the writer's aim and meaning in one out of two contiguous compositions, I shall deeply regret it.

Having at last, I think, finished with the personal points that I was recommended to notice, I will forsake the immediate object of this Preface; and, leaving *Late Lyrics* to whatever fate it deserves, digress for a few moments to more general considerations. The thoughts of any man of letters concerned to keep poetry alive cannot but run uncomfortably on the precarious prospects of English verse at the present day. Verily the hazards and casualties surrounding the birth and setting forth of almost every modern creation in numbers are ominously like those of one of Shelley's paper-boats on a windy lake. And a forward conjecture scarcely permits the hope of a better time, unless men's tendencies should change. So indeed of all art, literature, and 'high thinking' nowadays. Whether owing to the barbarising of taste in the younger minds by the dark madness of the late war, the unabashed cultivation of selfishness in all classes, the plethoric growth of knowledge simultaneously with the stunting of wisdom, 'a degrading thirst after outrageous stimulation' (to quote Wordsworth again), or from any other cause, we seem threatened with a new Dark Age.

I formerly thought, like other much exercised writers, that so far as literature was concerned a partial cause might be impotent or mischievous criticism; the satirising of individuality, the lack of whole-seeing in contemporary estimates of poetry and kindred work, the knowingness affected by junior reviewers, the overgrowth of meticulousness in their peerings for an opinion, as if it were a cultivated habit in them to scrutinise the tool-marks and be blind to the building, to hearken for the key-creaks and be deaf to the diapason, to judge the landscape by a nocturnal exploration with a flash-lantern. In other words, to carry on the old game of sampling the poem or drama by quoting the worst line or worst passage only, in ignorance or not of Coleridge's proof that a versification of any length neither can be nor ought to be all poetry; of reading meanings into a book that its author never dreamt of writing there. I might go on interminably.

But I do not now think any such temporary obstructions to be the cause of the hazard, for these negligences and ignorances, though they may have stifled a few true poets in the run of generations, disperse like stricken leaves before the wind of next week, and are no more heard of again in the region of letters than their writers themselves. No; we may be convinced that something of the deeper sort mentioned must be the cause.

In any event poetry, pure literature in general, religion — I include religion, in its essential and undogmatic sense, because poetry and religion touch each other, or rather modulate into each other; are, indeed, often but different names for the same thing — these, I say, the visible signs of mental and emotional life, must like all other things keep moving, becoming; even though at present, when belief in witches of Endor is displacing the Darwinian theory and 'the truth that shall make you free', men's minds appear, as above noted, to be moving backwards rather than on. I speak somewhat sweepingly, and should except many thoughtful writers in verse and prose; also men in certain worthy but small bodies of various denominations, and perhaps in the homely quarter where advance might have been the very least expected a few years back — the English Church — if one reads it rightly as showing evidence of 'removing those things that are shaken', in accordance with the wise Epistolary recommendation to the Hebrews. For since the historic and once august hierarchy of Rome some generation ago lost its chance of being the religion of the future by doing otherwise, and throwing over the little band of New Catholics who were making a struggle for continuity by applying the principle of evolution to their own faith, joining hands with modern science, and outflanking the hesitating English instinct towards liturgical restatement (a flank march which I at the time quite expected to witness, with the gathering of many millions of waiting agnostics into its fold); since then, one may ask, what other purely English establishment than the Church, of sufficient dignity and footing, with such strength of old association, such scope for transmutability, such architectural spell, is left in this country to keep the shreds of morality together?[1]

It may indeed be a forlorn hope, a mere dream, that of an alliance between religion, which must be retained unless the world is to perish, and complete rationality, which must come, unless also the world is to perish, by means of the interfusing effect of poetry — 'the breath and finer spirit of

[1] However, one must not be too sanguine in reading signs, and since the above was written evidence that the Church will go far in the removal of 'things that are shaken' has not been encouraging.

all knowledge; the impassioned expression of science', as it was defined by an English poet who was quite orthodox in his ideas. But if it be true, as Comte argued, that advance is never in a straight line, but in a looped orbit, we may, in the aforesaid ominous moving backward, be doing it *pour mieux sauter*, drawing back for a spring. I repeat that I forlornly hope so, notwithstanding the supercilious regard of hope by Schopenhauer, von Hartmann, and other philosophers down to Einstein who have my respect. But one dares not prophesy. Physical, chronological, and other contingencies keep me in these days from critical studies and literary circles

> Where once we held debate, a band
> Of youthful friends, on mind and art

(if one may quote Tennyson in this century). Hence I cannot know how things are going so well as I used to know them, and the aforesaid limitations must quite prevent my knowing henceforward.

I have to thank the editors and owners of *The Times*, *Fortnightly*, *Mercury*, and other periodicals in which a few of the poems have appeared for kindly assenting to their being reclaimed for collected publication.

T. H.

February 1922.

WINTER WORDS
IN VARIOUS MOODS AND METRES

['*Winter Words*', *though prepared for the press, would have undergone further revision, had the author lived to issue it on the birthday of which he left the number uninserted below.*]

INTRODUCTORY NOTE

So far as I am aware, I happen to be the only English poet who has brought out a new volume of his verse on his ... birthday, whatever may have been the case with the ancient Greeks, for it must be remembered that poets did not die young in those days.

This, however, is not the point of the present few preliminary words. My last volume of poems was pronounced wholly gloomy and pessimistic by reviewers — even by some of the more able class. My sense of the oddity of this verdict may be imagined when, in selecting them, I had been, as I thought, rather too liberal in admitting flippant, not to say farcical, pieces into the collection. However, I did not suppose that the licensed tasters had wilfully misrepresented the book, and said nothing, knowing well that they could not have read it.

As labels stick, I foresee readily enough that the same perennial inscription will be set on the following pages, and therefore take no trouble to argue on the proceeding, notwithstanding the surprises to which I could treat my critics by uncovering a place here and there to them in the volume.

This being probably my last appearance on the literary stage, I would say, more seriously, that though, alas, it would be idle to pretend that the publication of these poems can have much interest for me, the track having been adventured so many times before today, the pieces themselves have been prepared with reasonable care, if not quite with the zest of a young man new to print.

I also repeat what I have often stated on such occasions, that no harmonious philosophy is attempted in these pages — or in any bygone pages of mine, for that matter.

T. H.

NOTES

'She, to Him', I–IV, pp. 4–6.

These poems, together with 'Neutral Tones', are the
earliest included in this selection; they were written in
or before the summer of 1867 (*E.L.*, p. 71). Mrs. Hardy
calls them 'part of a much larger number which perished',
i.e. were subsequently rejected and destroyed by the poet.
To judge from the Shakespearean tone of these four sur-
vivors, the sequence as a whole was evidently inspired
by the sonnets of Shakespeare, which, with their crypto-
autobiographical tone and their frequent hints of a sexual
unhappiness bordering on despair, must have attracted
Hardy very greatly.

'To Lizbie Browne', p. 16.

Mrs. Hardy (*E.L.*, p. 33) mentions 'a gamekeeper's pretty
daughter, who won Hardy's admiration because of her
beautiful bay-red hair. But she despised him, as being
two or three years her junior, and married early. He
celebrated her later on as "Lizbie Browne".' Hardy was at
this time about sixteen years old. It will be seen that the
poem says nothing about her being the older of the two;
indeed, 'I should have thought Girls ripen fast' conveys
the suggestion of an older man watching a child turn
unexpectedly fast into a woman. So is a personal ex-
perience subtly rearranged in many of Hardy's poems.
Of course, writing many years later, he would remember
her youthfulness and forget his own.

'The Self-Unseeing', p. 23.

Hardy's father, a builder by trade, was an accomplished

violinist. Mrs. Hardy (*E.L.*, p. 18) writes that Hardy as a boy was 'of ecstatic temperament, extraordinarily sensitive to music, and among the endless jigs, hornpipes, reels, waltzes, and country-dances that his father played of an evening in his early married years, and to which the boy danced a *pas seul* in the middle of the room, there were three or four that always moved the child to tears, though he strenuously tried to hide them'.

This is a good example of the way a piece of biographical information provides an interesting sidelight on a poem, without being in any way essential. If we knew nothing of Hardy's father, or of the circumstances of his boyhood, we should still understand the poem perfectly; it contains within itself everything that is necessary. Perfect happiness, careless of before and after, is unselfconscious; we are happy without pausing to say to ourselves, 'This is happiness'; the contented young couple and the dancing child, contemplated in memory by the grave middle-aged man, seem in retrospect to have been 'looking away' from their blessings, not out of ingratitude but in sheer, candid thoughtlessness.

'A Trampwoman's Tragedy', p. 29.
Mrs. Hardy writes (*L.Y.*, pp. 92–93): 'In April of this year [1902] he was writing "A Trampwoman's Tragedy" — a ballad [*sic*] based on some local story of an event more or less resembling the incidents embodied, which took place between 1820 and 1830. Hardy considered this, upon the whole, his most successful poem.'

'A Church Romance', p. 39.
This sonnet is Hardy's imaginative reconstruction of his mother's first sight of his father — though, once again, the poem would be equally touching and felicitous if this fact were not established. Florence Emily Hardy tells us in *E.L.* (pp. 16–17): 'Mrs. Hardy once described him [i.e.

her husband] to her son as he was when she first set eyes
on him in the now removed west gallery of Stinsford
Church, appearing to her more travelled glance (she had
lived for a time in London, Weymouth, and other towns)
and somewhat satirical vision, "rather amusingly old-
fashioned, in spite of being decidedly good-looking —
wearing the blue swallow-tailed coat with gilt embossed
buttons then customary, a red and black flowered waist-
coat, Wellington boots, and French-blue trousers." Morn-
ing service must have been a more exciting affair in those
days, when the music was provided, not by an incon-
spicuous organist, but by a whole gallery of such gaily
dressed figures — "ardent, young and trim" indeed! No
wonder she "turned"!'

'The Convergence of the Twain', p. 45.

The liner *Titanic*, at that time the largest ship afloat,
struck an iceberg on her maiden voyage (2.20 a.m., 15
April 1912), and went down with the loss of 1,513 out of
the 2,224 people on board. Hardy's view of the matter
seems to have been that all the time the men were busy
building a liner, the 'Immanent Will' was equally busy
building an iceberg. Basically it is the same view of life
as we find in a novel like *Tess of the d'Urbervilles*: the
'President of the Immortals' was enjoying some 'sport'.

'Poems of 1912–13', pp. 51–63.

The nine poems in this selection are taken from a group
of twenty-one, all concerned with Hardy's emotions of
grief, nostalgia, and self-reproach after the death of his
first wife, Emma Hardy, in November 1912. These twenty-
one are by no means the only poems which deal directly
with the theme: it has been estimated that Hardy wrote
at least fifty of such poems in the twelve months follow-
ing Emma's death.

'Rain on a Grave', p. 54.

Emma Hardy's own reminiscences, *Some Recollections* (for details see 'Suggestions for Reading and Reference') contains this passage: 'I can quite well remember when I was three years old being taken a little way into the country to see daisies, as children are taken to see the sea; my surprise and joy were very great when I saw a whole field of them, I can never forget the ecstatic state it put me in.'

'After a Journey', p. 58.

In 1870, Hardy as a young architect was called in to advise on the restoration of the church of St. Juliot, near Boscastle, Cornwall. Arriving at the Rectory after his journey, he was met by Miss Emma Lavinia Gifford, sister of the Rector's young wife. An attraction immediately developed, and Hardy began making visits to St. Juliot as often as he was able — some two or three times a year — until he and Emma were married in 1874. On these visits, they would go for picnics in the countryside, to which she introduced him.

Cf. *Some Recollections*: 'I rode my pretty mare Fanny and he walked by my side and I showed him some of the neighbourhood — the cliffs, along the roads, and through the scattered hamlets, sometimes gazing down at the solemn small shores where the seals lived, coming out of great caverns very occasionally.'

'Heredity', p. 75.

From Hardy's Journal, 19 February, 1889: 'The story of a face which goes through three generations or more, would make a fine novel or poem of the passage of time. The differences in personality to be ignored.' Cf. *The Well-Beloved*.

'Logs on the Hearth', p. 83.

The sister alluded to is Hardy's elder sister, Mary.

'During Wind and Rain', p. 83.

The editors of *Some Recollections* have assembled a remarkably full set of biographical facts about this poem, which they print on pp. 67–68. The family was Emma Hardy's, the scene Plymouth, even the associations of a rainstorm with the loss of early happiness is there in a passage of the *Recollections*. As usual, these correspondences are interesting rather than essential. Douglas Brown's brilliant critical commentary on the poem (*Thomas Hardy*, pp. 147–52) is none the less illuminating for mentioning none of them.

'In Time of "The Breaking of Nations" ', p. 87.

From Hardy's Journal:

'I believe it would be said by people who knew me well that I have a faculty (possibly not uncommon) for burying an emotion in my heart or brain for forty years, and exhuming it at the end of that time as fresh as when interred. For instance, the poem entitled "The Breaking of Nations" contains a feeling that moved me in 1870, during the Franco-Prussian war, when I chanced to be looking at such an agricultural incident in Cornwall. But I did not write the verses till during the war with Germany in 1914, and onwards. Query: where was that sentiment hiding itself during more than forty years?'

'Voices from Things Growing in a Churchyard', p. 94.

This, as it happens, relates to Stinsford Churchyard. All the people mentioned were known to Hardy through local tradition; 'Fanny Hurd', whose real name was Hurden — but Hardy wanted a rhyme for 'bird' — was a schoolfellow of his, a delicate child who died in adolescence.

SUGGESTIONS FOR READING
AND REFERENCE

(Place of publication in each case is London)

Douglas Brown: *Thomas Hardy* ('Men and Books' Series)
Longmans, 1953.

This is the best short treatment of Hardy's work as a
whole. The chapter on his poetry makes all the essential
points.

Emma Hardy: *Some Recollections*, edited by Evelyn Hardy
and Robert Gittings. Oxford University Press, 1961.

Hardy discovered this manuscript among his wife's be-
longings after her death. It is an interesting and valuable
essay in reminiscence, offering many clues to those who
enjoy poetry better if they can set it in a framework of
fact; and also well worth reading for its own sake, for
Emma Hardy was an intelligent and sympathetic woman.
Hardy's second wife quoted some of it in the first of her
two biographical volumes (see below), in a copy obviously
supplied by Hardy himself and fairly heavily corrected
and emended by him. This book restores the original text
and supplies the gaps; it also points out specific points of
correspondence with the poems.

Florence Emily Hardy: *The Early Life of Thomas Hardy,
1840–1891.* Macmillan, 1928; *The Later Years of Thomas
Hardy, 1892–1928.* Macmillan, 1930. (Now available in
one volume: *The Life of Thomas Hardy, 1840–1928.*
Macmillan, 1962.)

It is now generally assumed that these two volumes were
largely composed by Hardy himself. They therefore have
the documentary interest of an autobiography and also
its subjective quality. An invaluable mine of facts, they
should be referred to rather than swallowed whole. In the

notes to this selection their titles are abbreviated to *E.L.* and *L.Y.* respectively.

Hermann Lea : *Thomas Hardy's Wessex*. Macmillan, 1913.

This pleasant volume, illustrated by numerous photographs, is in effect a guide-book to 'Wessex'. It establishes the real names of places for which Hardy made up his own names (these are not always one-to-one correspondences, as he would often make up a fictitious town or village using elements from two or three real ones), and also follows up every clue that might establish the locale of any poem, story or novel. Hermann Lea, though he had no pretensions as a literary critic, established these facts with great patience, often getting his information from Hardy himself.

F. B. Pinion : *A Hardy Companion*. Macmillan, 1968.
An indispensable guide to Hardy's novels, stories and poems illustrated with maps and photographs. Full descriptions of each work give the publishing history and any relevant biographical information : chapters are devoted to Hardy's views on religion, literature etc. and there is an invaluable extended alphabetical guide to people and places mentioned in the works.

The New Wessex Edition of the Poems of Thomas Hardy, edited by James Gibson. Macmillan, 1975.

The New Wessex Edition of the Stories of Thomas Hardy, edited by F. B. Pinion. Macmillan, 1975.

The New Wessex Edition of the Novels of Thomas Hardy : general editor P. N. Furbank. Macmillan, 1974–5 (see page 140).

INDEX OF FIRST LINES

THE NEW WESSEX EDITION
OF THE NOVELS
General Editor P. N. Furbank

Desperate Remedies
Introduction by Claudius Beatty

Far from the Madding Crowd
Introduction by John Bayley

The Hand of Ethelberta
Introduction by Robert Gittings

Jude the Obscure
Introduction by Terry Eagleton

A Laodicean
Introduction by Barbara Hardy

The Mayor of Casterbridge
Introduction by Ian Gregor

A Pair of Blue Eyes
Introduction by Ronald Blythe

The Return of the Native
Introduction by Derwent May

Tess of the d'Urbervilles
Introduction by P. N. Furbank

The Trumpet-Major
Introduction by Barbara Hardy

Two on a Tower
Introduction by F. B. Pinion

Under the Greenwood Tree
Introduction by Geoffrey Grigson

The Well-Beloved
Introduction by J. Hillis Miller

The Woodlanders
Introduction by David Lodge